The

Corporation

and the

Economy

Notes by
W. H. FERRY
Followed by a Discussion

GREENWOOD PRESS, PUBLISHERS
WESTPORT, CONNECTICUT

Library of Congress Cataloging in Publication Data

Center for the Study of Democratic Institutions.
   The corporation and the economy.

      Reprint of the ed. published by Center for the Study
   of Democratic Institutions, Santa Barbara, Calif.
      1. Corporations. I. Ferry, W. H. II. Title.
   [HD2731.C4 1974]   338.7'4   73-16868
   ISBN 0-8371-7241-1

Originally published in 1959 by Center for the Study of
Democratic Institutions, Santa Barbara

Reprinted with the permission of W.H. Ferry

Reprinted in 1974 by Greenwood Press,
a division of Williamhouse-Regency Inc.

Library of Congress Catalogue Card Number 73-16868

ISBN 0-8371-7241-1

Printed in the United States of America

FOREWORD The following *Notes* represent a kind of distillation of the work and findings of the people who have been engaged for the past year and a half in studying the Corporation under the basic issues program of the Fund for the Republic. The program is now being carried on at the Center for the Study of Democratic Institutions, which the Fund has established in Santa Barbara, California.

W. H. Ferry, who is Vice President of the Fund and the staff administrator of the Corporation Project, based his *Notes* on the studies that have been prepared for the Project, the conferences held by the Advisory Committee to the Project, and the meetings of a Seminar on the Corporation organized by Scott Buchanan.

The *Notes* were discussed by the staff almost daily over a two-week period and the final draft that resulted from these discussions was presented to the Consultants for two days of discussion on April 26 and 27, 1959. It is this draft which is printed here. It is followed by an edited version of the Consultants' remarks.

The participants in the April meetings were: A. A. Berle, Jr., Scott Buchanan, Eric Goldman, Clark Kerr, John Courtney Murray, S.J., Reinhold Niebuhr, and I. I. Rabi, *Consultants*; Robert M. Hutchins, who served as chairman of the meetings; John Cogley, W. H. Ferry, Hallock Hoffman, Paul Jacobs, Frank K. Kelly, Walter Millis, James Real, and Edward Reed, of the staff.

Notes

THE ARGUMENT

1. The "economy" is that part of the activity of the citizens which produces and distributes the goods and services required by society.

2. The economy is subsidiary to society, which has ends in addition to its economic ends.

3. The economy must serve the general welfare.

4. The economy serves the general welfare by producing the goods and services required by it under conditions assuring their just and rational production and their just and equitable distribution.

5. The society has the power and authority to state the ends and conditions that are to be met by the economy. Allocations of wealth and energy must be made in terms of the general welfare.

6. No generally accepted and rational theory exists for the accomplishment of these objects.

7. Whatever mechanisms and controls are necessary to hold the economy to its proper purposes, and to make the men and associations who have power in the economy accountable, are

5

just and proper. This includes formal planning by the national government designed to protect and promote the general welfare. The public has the right to know who is in charge, what they are doing, and what the consequences of their actions may be. When these conditions are met, the economy can claim to be serving the general welfare.

8. The private *organization* of economic enterprise, involving as it does great parts of the lives of all the citizens, must also conform to the standards of justice and freedom that society establishes. The typical economic organization, the corporation, is in its nature a "private" government; it has public effects and the effects on those governed and on the public alike need disinterested and systematic appraisal.

9. Technology imposes novel demands upon both the economic organizations and society as a whole. The implications of technology for the future are overwhelming. Its direction and its most significant products should be brought under public control.

THE thread linking the following observations is that of corporate power: the use being made of it at present, the uses to which it might be put, and how desirable changes might be made. Corporate power is taken to mean the ability or capacity to enforce decisions affecting large numbers of people. This is a definition of trade union power and of political power as well. There are three principal methods of dealing with power, corporate or other, and each has its place. One is to take it away; another is to regulate, control, or call it to account; and the last is to put it into competition with other powers.

The Bill of Rights is the principal protection the citizen has against arbitrary or capricious exercise of political power. When these ten amendments were being considered, two main arguments were advanced against their adoption. The first was that they were unnecessary because the Constitution itself provided the protection, even though by implication. The second said that protections should be developed as needed, in the tradition of Magna Carta and the common law in which most Americans of that time had been reared.

Nonetheless, the Bill of Rights was ratified. The argument prevailed that a central government's potential capacity to suppress liberty and justice was such that it would do no harm to have the boundaries of its actions clearly marked. The ratifiers did not regard government or the people in it as villainous. They merely sought to deal before the event with immense power, almost at the moment that they were confiding the future of the nation to this very power.

The main thread of these observations, as the Argument suggests, is joined with a proposition that the corporation is not an end in itself but merely the most useful device that an industrial society has developed to achieve certain of its important ends. It is assumed that the corporation is still in a period of growth, with the probability that decided alterations in its relations to government and the rest of the community will occur; and that the society has the right to decide on the main lines of change.

There is little doubt that the values in American life today are largely those of the corporation. A question is raised whether this is the proper order of things, and whether it would not be preferable for society to establish values to which the corporation might be expected to contribute and to conform. As the most important single factor in the lives of most Americans, the corporation should be required to make affirmative contributions to freedom and justice as our distinguishing values.

A bias in favor of the corporation as a profit-making institution will be observed throughout this paper. This bias includes a fear that the business corporation's essential genius, that of organizing collective effort to make money, is being diluted in ways that have questionable worth. A great deal more is heard these days about social responsibility and corporate duties toward the community than about the profit function. We see the corporation simultaneously becoming a political aggregation, a family, and a welfare organization, activities that do not necessarily fit a profit-making enterprise.

This proliferation may work against the best interests both of the corporation and of the country. There is no evidence to indicate, for example, that the corporation has special competence to mix into the educational process, or to substitute its "conscience" for that of people affected by it, or to set cultural levels for the nation.

The corporation that makes a reasonable profit for its owners by making a good product and selling it at a reasonable price, while paying just wages to employees, warrants the favorable opinion and backing of the community without other evidences of "good citizenship." There are certain standards of civilized behavior that the profit-bent corporation would not ignore; for example, it would not litter the streams, streets, or atmosphere. But the observation of such standards is no more a *raison d'être* for the corporation than meeting the ordinary requirements of citizenship is the reason for personal existence.

Adolf A. Berle, Jr., and others foresee drastic changes in the corporation and in the economy. Mr. Berle forecasts a rapid evolution toward greater "public accountability"; toward an economy even more mixed that it is at present, with government intervening to secure a better balance between public and private production; and toward limitation of the power of giant industrial complexes over individuals and groups by application of Constitutional concepts and other means. These *Notes* rely heavily on the words of Lincoln: "The dogmas of the quiet past are inadequate for the stormy present. We must think anew, we must act anew, we must disenthrall ourselves."

The need for a new theory

The goals of the corporation are no longer clear. The profit function is only one of many. The slogans by which the corporation lives are more ritual than reality. The conventional wisdom says that uncontrolled enterprise is the economic key to the general welfare; but enterprise is most free in the medium-sized companies and on the peripheries of industry, in the small, local, and retail businesses. As the number of stockholders grows, the old ideas of private property alter and become dim. The myth of the Market as a self-regulating mechanism still reigns, though it does not work and is not expected to work in large sectors, for example steel and autos; and despite evidence that it cannot be depended on to produce a stable society, much less a just one.

New theory is needed to dispel the ghosts of Adam Smith, Marshall, and their successors. E. S. Mason observes: "The attack on the capitalist apologetic of the Nineteenth Century has been successful but a satisfactory contemporary apologetic is still to be created." We are well into the Era of the Giant Corporation, which, it is clearly seen, is not just the individual economic unit writ large, working through the Invisible Hand to maximize the welfare of all. There is no theory of the firm that satisfactorily explains or justifies the large modern corporation. Efforts are made to elevate the idea of social responsibility (or, synonymously, the corporate conscience or good citizenship) to the status of a theory of the firm.

Andrew Hacker has argued that this development contains doubtful and antisocial seeds, because it arrogates to the corporations powers belonging to the individual or to the government. Theodore Levitt and others propose that the corporation make the profit function its sole concern, with all other activities to be justified by this standard. Their argument is that this need not entail ruthless or antisocial behavior, though it does require a refreshed public understanding of the place of the corporation in society. None would gain so much from an adequate theory of the firm, based on profit-making, as the corporation itself. In permitting public judgment by other criteria, the corporation is needlessly and perilously exposing itself. The corporation, it is noted, often justifies its "conscientious" behavior as a calculated effort to ward off political intervention in both the long and the short term, in this way relating all such activities to future profit-making.

There need be no regret that obsolete theories are crumbling. The confusion is forcing much needed reflection on what is happening and to what end.

The need for criticism

New institutional arrangements are needed to assist in the formulation of political-economic theory and to provide organized and disinterested appraisal of the corporation and the economic machinery. This critical effort should be private, and should be instituted by collaboration between universities and foundations. Criticism of the corporation and the economic machinery at present is partisan, disorganized, and partial. One reason for this is that the traditional agencies of criticism—the press, the universities, the churches—have themselves secured vested interests in the economic machine. Another reason is that criticism of economic institutions is readily equated with un-American ideas. A third is that criticism has difficulty in making itself heard in a period of affluence and national self-satisfaction.

The first tasks of an agency of criticism would be the establishment of aims for the economy and the development of standards of corporate performance. For example, a declaration that the purpose of the economic system is to supply goods in adequate amounts, at reasonable prices, and in a just manner might suffice to open the discussion concerning proper aims. The impartial agency would seek to measure performance against the traditional aims of the republic, a kind of measurement not now being made in any quarter. An analogy may be seen in the various university law reviews, to which the courts are sensitive. This example suggests that a critical agency should be "official" in the sense, for example, that the Harvard, Yale, or Columbia Law Reviews are "official." An institutional scheme for respected and "official" criticism of the corporation and economic order will call for inventiveness and patience.

Corporation managers argue that there is too much criticism already. They suggest that Big Business is a political whipping boy at least every four years and often between elections, too, and that this is enough to ask anyone to endure. But the object of criticism by a disinterested group would be not political attack but public improvement. It might, for example, help to distinguish the proper responsibilities of the public and private sectors. It might report on the relation that size bears to efficiency. It might obtain objective evidence about the impact of corporate life on the lives of employees. It might clarify the much-debated proposal that consolidated financial reports be broken down so that consumers can see how much of the price they pay for car A, for example, goes to cover losses in the production and sale of car B. It might weigh the effects of corporate contributions to education. It might consider the gains and losses to freedom and justice in an oligarchically controlled business structure. It might tackle the incentives and rewards system with a view to determining whether the present method of executive compensation works for or against the public interest. J. A. Livingston and others argue that present levels of compensation and perquisites in private business practically assure that government (including education) will never be able to recruit the devotion and brains the country is entitled to have in its classrooms and offices.

The foregoing suggests that whatever harm is done to freedom and justice by the corporation is a symptom. The ailment is to be found in the aims of society. The community appears to care more for Westerns and fintail cars than it does for freedom and justice. It seems to show little disposition to worry about the providers thereof, beyond giving an approving round of applause once in a while to the Anti-Trust Division. This paper nevertheless proceeds on the conviction that Americans seek better standards and liberty and justice, and that by education and criticism a rational, free, and prosperous society can be achieved.

A critical agency would make a start, in short, at clarifying the aims of the economy. At the same time it would seek to raise new standards of accountability. Power pyramids in American life are viewed with suspicion, as is seen in the efforts to legislate accountability into the power pyramids of the trade unions. Corporate pyramids pose a different conundrum to democratic theory. Their accountability is limited and private. It amounts on the one hand to obeying the law and on the other to programs to "present the company's story" to stockholders, employees, and others. Such efforts amount to only partial accountability. They do not necessarily show how the corporation may be meeting the needs of society, as judged by criteria established by the community and not by itself. The great debate over steel prices, wages, and inflation is a measure of the current groping for accountability. We know that a union which is democratically and legally run can at the same time be socially irresponsible. The performance of the corporation must similarly be assessed on public grounds as well as those of its own choosing. The concern is not with misdeeds but with power. Power must be used—even non-use is a kind of use—and present modes of accountability are not adequate to the growth and concentration of corporate power.

The idea of public accountability is old. Louis Hartz and Oscar Handlin show that it was a conspicuous and central feature of state-business relations before the Civil War. "Too often the absence of activity by the federal government has been taken for the absence of all activity, the denial of its right to act, the denial of the right of any government to act." As the several states struggled toward economic maturity and sought to make the best use of their resources, they established systems of public accountability. The belief that until recently the country had everywhere pursued strict laissez faire policies is without foundation. Governmental controls, accountability, and industry-state cooperation are an old story in the United States.

The need for constitutionalization

The process of "constitutionalizing the corporation" is at the verge of significant developments. These are likely to proceed along two lines. The first is in the direction of formal constitutions for the internal government of the corporation. Such a constitution would seek to define the rights and responsibilities of the members of the organization. The corporate constitution might not look like the constitution of government, and need not necessarily be concerned with such matters as representation and participation. Some argue that the corporation cannot be constitutionally governed, because of doubt that profits can be made or efficiency achieved. Others argue that profits and efficiency are not the only desiderata, that a way must be found to make the corporation genuinely responsive to its members, and that the power of the organization over members requires formal and effective checks. (Who the members of a corporation are is a tidy question. Once only the "owners"—the stockholders—were so considered. But now employees appear to have been admitted to membership; and some political scientists would add consumers. The expanded notion of membership is aided by modern management's view of itself as steward not of the owners but of the interests of all groups.)

The other line of constitutional development is from the outside, and includes judicial decisions of more and more scope concerning the rights of individuals to be free of discriminatory practices by the corporation. Concepts of procedural and substantive due process to cover corporate acts are being liberalized, aimed at keeping exercise of corporate power within the limits set by the Bill of Rights and the Fourteenth Amendment.

A more or less planned economy

Corporate behavior, however important, is still a secondary question. The primary issue is that of the political economy. The old view of politics and economics occupying separate domains has gone forever. Today we have an economic system inextricably intermingled with a political system, and a political system with inescapable duties to promote the general welfare through the economic order. A. A. Berle and others emphasize that in this area the debate is moving to a decisive phase. The poles of the debate are more planning or less planning by government; and those favoring more planning, together with those who regard it as inevitable, are becoming more articulate every day. Senator

Hubert Humphrey recently suggested that national planning was the only reasonable way to deal with today's immense problems.

The idea of countervailing power does not appear as forceful as it once did as a rationale for economic order. For it is seen that while countervailing power might achieve an equilibrium, it does not necessarily move matters along at the right speed or produce the right things in socially desirable quantities. It is a theory of happy accidents, and perhaps a good way to explain what has been happening in economic life. But that it and related theories are not necessarily reliable formulas for the future can be observed in the way management and labor in some industries are learning to cut the pie together at the expense of the consumer; in the change in the make-up of the labor force; in the Defense Department-Big Business complex; and in the warm relations between regulators and regulatees. There is also the important fact that American confidence in the economic machine as an uniquely effective way to mobilize large groups of people for common ends has been roughly shaken by Russia.

More and more we are asking whether it is possible to organize matters better—perhaps with planning as a central means—to serve the ends of a liberal republic. Contemporary concern with what these ends may actually be is exemplified by the recent appointment of a Presidential Commission on National Goals.

The idea of planning by central authority in the United States has to contend with many dubious and even sinister connotations. This is somewhat anomalous in the light of the high place given to planning elsewhere in the community. There is no such thing as an unplanned corporation; indeed, efficiency and profitability are closely associated with the idea of planning. The State Department has a Policy Planning Staff; unions and trade associations, school boards and farm bureaus have planning and coordinating committees. There are metropolitan and tri-state planning agencies for traffic and river control and bridge and port construction, and there is a federal super-highway plan. Perhaps the success of planning at these lower levels is doing something to temper the opposition that suggestions of central planning up to now have evoked.

Lincoln's dictum was that the government should do what the people need to have done but cannot do or do as well by individual effort. Providing for the common defense is one thing that the people cannot do for themselves, and there is no objection to the vast planning this demands. There are numerous other tasks that the people cannot do on their own, even through their most powerful local or non-governmental institutions. These include the prudent allocation and conservation of resources; a sound development of agriculture; the control of recession, inflation, and unemployment; aid to social and economic development in other countries; and securing a rational balance between production of public goods and services (highways, hospitals, parks, education, libraries) and private production (television sets, automobiles, cosmetics, toys, cigarettes, and the rest).

Obtaining a consensus on national planning would require:

- That the need for it be clearly demonstrated;

- That the grip on the country's imagination of obsolete ideas such as a totally self-regulating market be loosened by patient argument;

- That the advice of the many public and private agencies experienced in planning—including that of corporations and unions—be solicited;

- That national planning be accomplished by statute, not by executive order, and that the legislation include provision for enforcement;

- That planning be given official stature commensurate with its responsibilities, perhaps by making the chairman of the national planning agency a Cabinet officer;

- That unequivocal guarantees of political liberty be written into its charter.

National planning should be undertaken not as an anti-corporate or anti-private property measure, but as a logical evolution demanded by the increasing complexity of modern life.

Planning should not result in regimentation of economic activity, nor the elimination of amenities, luxuries, or even trivialities. Planning that comes about through legislative (as contrasted with executive) action should offer some guarantee against such results.

The situation today presents a strong argument for planning. All of the conventional signs of prosperity are present. The stock market is at a record peak, and so is the gross national product. With grumbling but without pain the country is meeting a near 80-billion-dollar national budget, including a 40-billion-dollar expenditure on arms. A record number of new companies is opening shop. The market is overrunning with every kind of commodity and service. We are growing far more than we can eat. Our goods and wealth are in demand throughout the world. Yet this surfeit is accomplished while one-fifth of the national productive machinery stands unused, while unemployment persists at a high level, while food surpluses burst out of government bins, and while humanity elsewhere is starving.

National planning is the sensible way of trying to resolve these fateful paradoxes, unless a better method can be found. In such circumstances the "self-regulating" economy seems to be a doubtful prescription,[1] and one to which the country has already shown its unwillingness fully to entrust its future.

When Congress voted the Employment Act of 1946, it put the government permanently in the planning business by authorizing federal action whenever the possibility of depression and mass unemployment appeared. Many have pointed out that there are in fact dozens of official agencies already engaged in planning. What is missing is coherent policy and coordination.

---

[1] Commenting on the chaotic "urban sprawl" of Greater New York and the impending catastrophe unless something is done about it, *The New York Times* said: "The problem is . . . what treatment is required. . . . Even if all elements in our society were agreed on a unified solution—which is by no means the case —the political means for its realization might still prove inadequate. One notable lack in the whole picture would appear to be leadership. . . . No plan, project, or program designed to meet the totality of the challenge has yet emerged. It is the familiar story of man's greater talent for creating machines than for creating systems that will make the machine his creature rather than his master."

The spectre of an all-powerful planning agency can be eliminated, for it is inconceivable that Congress would authorize any such thing. The choice is not between complete planning and complete laissez faire. Between these extremes is a middle ground with a multitude of possibilities, many unexplored. The future of national planning would in fact seem most likely to be the sum of the efforts in this middle ground of a host of agencies — public, semi-public, and private.[2]

One might speculate, for example, as to how planning might be brought into the automobile industry. The plans of its managers undeniably have a great deal to do with the behavior of the economy, and none publicly denied the headline of a few years ago, "As Detroit Goes, So Goes the Nation." The auto industry has an elaborate strategy which centers around planned obsolescence, annual model changes, installment buying, and administered pricing.

The effects of the industry on the market and on the mores are incalculable. It uses vast amounts of manpower and materials. The allocation of materials in potentially short supply has always affected it powerfully, as in 1942-45. With regard to matters within the industry's own control, it is at least conceivable that at some point it might decide that it was bearing rather more responsibility for the national well-being than it wished to bear. Presuming that difficulties with the anti-trust laws could be avoided, the industry might decide to engage in some self-regulation, if only to forestall federal controls. Self-regulation, or voluntary planning, could take many different forms. It could be based on a strategy far different from the present one; for example, that of providing sensible and safe transportation at a fair price and in the expectation of a steady and satisfactory profit. To carry out this strategy the industry might establish a board of self-regulators. One of the board's first

---

[2] Bertrand de Jouvenel says the state-industry situation in France has "melted" in recent years: "Civil servants, directors of public corporations, and directors of private corporations more and more sit down together in round tables to discuss conditions and their future operations. I regard [this] as an 'open conspiracy' for the public weal."

steps might be industry-wide agreement that a new model would be brought on the market only when it could be demonstrated to the satisfaction of the voluntary planning group that the new model differed significantly from models then in production. It might be expected to meet one of three tests:

1) That the new model was significantly cheaper to build and therefore able to be sold at a significantly lower price; 2) that it was significantly cheaper to operate; or 3) that it contained significant functional improvements.

This is an extreme suggestion, one that goes against current practice and basic belief and hence one that would produce violent reaction. Would such a step solve more problems than it raised? There is no reason to think that it would diminish competition. It would not reduce the total supply of auto transportation. Automobiles might be sold because of real need rather than because of needs stimulated by annual changeovers and heavy advertising. It might make the industry more stable and therefore leave the country less at its economic mercy than seems to be the case at present. It might result in technological improvements making for safer and more economical travel, and in alleviating some of the problems of highway construction, parking, and general strangulation that confront the country everywhere.

On the other hand, voluntary planning might have none of these effects. The cure might be worse than the ailment. What would happen to employment, and to the industries, from oil companies to advertising to parts suppliers, that depend on the present strategy? Would planning aggravate the tendency to monopoly that has always been looked on so suspiciously? If the auto industry is so central to the economy, should it not be subject not to self-regulation but to formal controls, as are the utilities and railroads?

Another approach, this time as an example of public planning, might be to establish lines of demarcation in those major industries around which the economic fortunes of the country revolve. The object would be to place companies of a certain size or strategic importance to the general welfare on one side of the line where they would be subject to specific legal restraints and public accountability. On the other side of the line would be all other companies, which would be free to operate as they chose. The location of the line would differ in every industry, but the aim would be the same, the control of national boat-rocking by private enterprise, and a more prudent use of natural and human resources. Companies would be free to decide to which group they wanted to belong. If they elected to operate below the line, they could do so by taking steps to meet the criteria for this group. This might mean divesting themselves of certain activities, and taking care not to acquire again the economic power of members of the above-the-line group. Others might elect to operate above the line, thereby acknowledging their economic influence and consenting to observe the practices and standards of accountability appropriate to organizations so intimately bound up with the general welfare. This need not result in a public utility kind of regulation, and indeed there is no reason to think that this would be necessary. Dim hints of some such line of demarcation already lurk behind anti-trust policy, as can be seen in certain of the pleadings in the proceedings recently instituted against General Motors. Making a formal distinction as to companies "affecting the general welfare" would merely be recognizing and making visible an already existing state of affairs.

Today's mixed economy is characterized by much regulation and many cooperative arrangements, a number of the most successful of them recommended by the National Planning Association, which was founded in 1934 and has survived many vicissitudes to remain planning's most effective spokesman. Through numerous studies of local and national problems it has demonstrated the utility of planning on many levels. This is not to intimate that the NPA has supported central planning on the lines argued above, but to indicate the support that planning already enjoys. NPA, with businessmen prominent on its board, has shown the way to many of the regional and local schemes that involve business-union-government cooperation.

At the same time there is, as has been seen, no name for this mixed system and little effective theory. The discussion is seriously impeded by obsolete and almost irrelevant terms like socialism and capitalism. The terms of the discussion are misleading in their historical assumptions as well as in their application of Eighteenth Century economic ideas to Twentieth Century realities. For many years corporations were chartered expressly to do the will of the state. Their continuation depended on their performance in meeting the "demands of the public welfare." Many kinds of enterprise, from wholly-owned public works to mixed corporations with public and private directors, were chartered to take fullest advantage of resources and to meet competition.[3]

Planning should be considered also in relation to the sharp argument about national economic growth. At present the rate of growth is a result perceived after the event, a mathematical calculation of economic history. Yet it may be assumed that there is a desirable rate of economic development, and that it is possible to determine this rate. Many of the factors in such a determination are well-established: the growth of the population; the needs of the common defense; a rising standard of living for all; increasing demands that can be met only by public action—for schools, slum clearance, etc.—and U. S. obligations to less fortunate nations.

But there is no agency charged with bringing together and weighing all the factors,[4] and thereby perhaps establishing an

---

[3] "Corporations originally were regarded as agencies of the state. . . . A corporation, therefore, may be defined in the light of history as a body created by law for the purpose of attaining public ends through an appeal to private interests. . . . We cannot consent to the opinion that a corporation can be a purely private affair. . . . The logical development of this early idea would have resulted in the enforcement of a strict accountability to the state, which we at present lack. . . ." Henry Carter Adams and L. S. Rowe, in *Relation of the State to Industrial Action and Economics and Jurisprudence,* Jos. Dorfman, editor. Columbia University Press, 1954.

[4] A National Resources Planning Board emerged in 1939 from a consolidation of various New Deal planning commissions and committees. It was created by Executive Order and expired in 1943 for lack of funds. Despite the difficulties with Congress with which it was always struggling, the NRPB produced a number of remarkable studies, many of which contributed markedly to late

"optimum" rate. And if there were such an agency the crucial question would still remain, by what methods is the optimum rate of growth to be achieved? Who does what for whom? Is it possible or desirable to "enforce" an optimum rate of national growth? Would it be better to leave growth to the theory of happy accidents, aided by occasional nudges of federal fiscal policy? This is the line the country is most often urged to follow.[5] The persuasive arguments for it are based on history and do not take account of the dense texture of today's society and the interdependence of all parts of the community.

(continued from page 20)

New Deal and early World War II policies. One of the last of these was called *Security, Work, and Relief Policies,* which contained the following "New Bill of Rights": (1) Right to work usefully and creatively through the productive years. (2) The right to fair pay, adequate to command the necessities and amenities of life in exchange for work, ideas, thrift, and other socially valuable service. (3) The right to adequate food, clothing, shelter, and medical care. (4) The right to security, with freedom from fear of old age, want, dependency, sickness, unemployment, and accident. (5) The right to live in a system of free enterprise, free from compulsory labor, irresponsible private power, arbitrary public authority, and unregulated monopolies. (6) The right to come and go, to speak and to be silent, free from spying of secret police. (7) The right to equality before the law, with equal access to justice in fact. (8) The right to education, for work, for citizenship, and for personal growth and happiness. (9) The right to rest, recreation, and adventure, the opportunity to enjoy and take part in an advancing civilization.

[5] "In a free society protected against violence and fraud, economic growth is an automatic process. . . . No arbitrary rate can be postulated and treated as a national objective. This is where the sloganeers of 'economic growth' are treading on dangerous ground. To them, economic growth is not merely a natural and desirable occurrence; it is a program. They would set up a goal based upon theoretical calculations rather than practical experience, and . . . would make use of fiscal policy, monetary policy, and various forms of centralized planning. . . . It is significant that businessmen are seldom found among the proponents or adherents of such schemes. . . . The desirability of economic growth is not subject to question, and if the United States can achieve a long-term annual growth rate of 5 per cent or even more, so much the better. But when economic growth becomes a slogan for proposals aimed at uninterrupted business boom, it becomes a menace to economic stability and economic freedom as well." *The Guaranty Survey,* March 1959. Guaranty Trust Co., New York.

As the nation moves daily into closer contact with the rest of the world the need for a systematic—i.e., a planned—approach to questions of far-reaching consequences becomes urgent. The fragmentation of foreign aid activities and their ambiguous relations to one another and to private enterprise are now clearly a critical weakness. A move toward coherent planning of foreign aid is to be seen in the recommendation of a Presidential Commission that all foreign economic programs be brought under a single agency. The agency would also be "concerned with assuring that private enterprise is used as fully as possible." A strong component of a national plan would be found in the adoption of some such recommendations as these.

Technology and bureaucracy

Technology is the lifeblood of the economic system, as bureaucracy is its nervous system. Technology, taken to mean organized knowledge and techniques, is neutral; that is, it is value-free, and its products can be used for general good as for general ill. Technology is a common resource, and the dominant fact of our lives. We choose to have it this way, and under-developed nations see technology as the only desirable line for them to take. In writing its own rules it writes many at the same time for society. Changes in tools and techniques produce violent changes in political and social relationships. It has been observed that military policy is decided by weapons technology, and not vice versa. Dramatic as fusion-fission technology may be, it is nevertheless only one of many developments that are sure to effect drastic transformations in the human condition. Geneticists appear to be on the way to discovering thoroughbred mating, so that we can if we will obtain a standard quality of human being. Biochemistry has already produced elementary forms of life. None can yet tell whether throwing a radiation belt around the world is a great benefit or a precursor of disaster. Tranquilizers will be succeeded by happiness pills and doubtless unhappiness pills. Already technology is producing spectacular alterations in society; one thinks of the effects wrought by television and automation in little more than a decade. These are collective, not occasional and individual, effects. The question would seem to be, what do we need to do to live with the knowledge now coming into our possession?

History is not of much help in answering the absolutely novel questions posed by technology. Some kind of public appraisal, planning, and control of the most powerful, dangerous, and influential products of technology would appear to be indispensable. The imagination is staggered by such a notion. We have been used to thinking of technology as a positive good that should be allowed to develop unhindered by any restraints except perhaps those of the market.

Despite the immensity and intricacy of the task, the control of technology still appears possible, even though unlikely. Private and public organizations show us some of the methods of cooperation and direct control that may have to be called on. Du Pont often publicizes its Chart Room, where decisions are made about the rate at which the company's technological innovations are to be permitted to flow into the market. Here plans are also made to assure that the market is ready and receptive. Weather ships under international control dot the oceans, and are an integral part of world-wide meteorology. The International Labor Office facilitates the exchange of information on the effects of automation and other technology affecting working people.

Out of such examples it may be possible to erect the rudiments of a control system. Public appraisal of the potential social utility of technological advances—perhaps by an agency like the one described earlier—would appear to be needed immediately. It can scarcely be doubted that appraisal of automation might have considerably eased its impact, and might even now allow us to deal with its implications for a free and decent society far better than we are doing. "We are in danger of forgetting the principles of political liberty in our concern to keep the machines running."

Bureaucracy is a necessary condition of an "industrializing" society, and indeed of any large organization from the Post Office to the trade union to the fraternal organization. Well over 80 per cent of those gainfully employed off the farms are in corporations, large and small. Corporation life, as factory worker, bureaucrat, or manager, is the common destiny of Americans.

The progress made by the economic order in conquering the forms and methods of bureaucracy has been brilliant. But the result of bureaucracy is a different question. Where the factory employee is concerned, the problem is one of work, its satisfactions and discontents, and of his union or lack of one. For that great group of men and women now in transition between blue collar and white collar the change of status brings new satisfactions and new perplexities. For the first time there is the possibility of the widespread "enjoyment of work," with few suggestions however as to how to achieve it. (Many in fact argue just the other way; that work is an insoluble problem, "enjoyment of work" is a contradiction, and most work is necessarily mean, monotonous, and arduous; and in any case technology, by bringing the 20- or 24-hour week, will make it of minimal importance, soon to be replaced by the problem of leisure.)

While automation and other advances herald a stepping-up of the skilled groups, there is yet no chance of "return to personal craftsmanship." The new technology may enable some workers to escape the grinding routines of the factory. There will still remain the problem of finding in work something worth doing for its own sake. Over the past two generations trade union activity has brought pay and fringe benefits and conditions of work to remarkable heights. Now the unions are starting to worry about whether the industrial machinery of the nation can or should be geared to produce larger quantities of satisfaction, together with a sense of freedom and justice, for those participating in it.

Where the white-collar employee—bureaucrat and manager— is concerned, the problem is that of *anomie*. With the best will in the world many managers are struggling with the facelessness of corporate life. How successful they are depends on the standards that are used. Decentralization has, for example, meant more authority for more men. But company security systems and pensions and other benefits tend to lock many more into their jobs. There is, moreover, devotion to the proposition that the welfare of the employee and that of the employer are identical. There is little disagreement with Andrew Hacker's point that for a variety of reasons the corporate employee's primary commitments are to his company and not to his community or even to his own self-development.

As troublesome a question as any is how a sense of individual worth and dignity may be made of compelling importance to a bureaucratic population that shows little sign of prizing these qualities.[6] It is hard to tell how seriously this should be regarded. There seems to be a general deploring of the just-graduated job-seeker who inquires about pension plans before he inquires about the opportunities. This is seen as an indication that self-reliance and the adventurous spirit are on the wane. But corporations, farmers, and college teachers pursue security just as diligently in ways that are familiar to everyone.

Almost all the forces playing on the individual today tend to push him away from himself and toward bureaucracy. There is the lack of connection he feels between political decisions on great issues and his own opinions. He feels controlled rather than controlling. There is the Bomb which, so far as he knows, may put an end to his universe any moment. There is the sense of irresponsibility and anonymity that goes with working in large organizations. Television puts *Gunsmoke* and Sergeant Bilko between him and fierce problems. He sees that the non-controversial man seems to get ahead faster than the controversial man. Teachers say that they are more concerned about adjusting his children to the community than they are about educating them.

Attempts are being made to bring personality back into the economic and corporate structure. These include suggestions that employees ought to have more freedom than they now have to schedule their own workloads, and for the extension of profit-

---

[6] Many, including most corporate spokesmen, disagree sharply with this view. See especially *The Uncommon Man,* by Crawford H. Greenewalt, McGraw-Hill, New York, 1959.

sharing schemes and other devices designed to give employees a sense of participation in common tasks. While all such efforts are to be encouraged, the main hope would appear to lie in schemes and innovations of the kind discussed earlier: critical attention to the real aims of corporation and economy.

THE American corporation is prospering as the typical form of organization in mid-Twentieth Century. Its species multiply, its achievements widen, its paradoxes become sharper. To the casual observer things have never been more right with either corporation or economic system than they are at present. The corporation carries the burden of production and plenty for the affluent society. Its schemes for employees are models even for socialist rivals. Doing business with government, for years regarded as a natural enemy, is a necessary condition of existence which the corporation has learned to accept with grace and profit. It is a factor of no mean dimensions in lightening the worker's load and opening new perspectives of economic freedom to him. Warm truce rather than cold war is the corporation's customary relation with organized employees. For the unorganized it has human relations programs constantly growing in coverage and scope.

Its economic power is vast, but not "constrained by the market nor by any recognizable or explicit standard." It does not agree that the exercise of corporate power should be accompanied by some recognized and accepted form of restraint. It says no restraint except self-restraint is needed because it is conscientious, its outlook is benign, and its actions are at one with the general welfare. It considers it has the right to do business where it cares to abroad, except perhaps behind the Iron Curtain. This self-conferred ambassadorial status is creating difficulties in many important sections of the world.

The corporation appears, finally, to enjoy the anomalies of its position. It is not keen for criticism, least of all from those outside the corporate walls. But the corporation bulks far larger in the life of the mid-Twentieth Century American than even the central government did in the life of the late Eighteenth Century American. The problems of the large corporation and the economy are problems of the common domain. Discussion, criticism, education, and planning all have their part to play in stimulating the corporation and the economic system to maximum usefulness in a society based on freedom and justice.

A Discussion

FERRY: I am aware of many things that are not mentioned in the paper. This includes such important topics as methods for restraining inflation and encouraging growth of the gross national product, the economic effects of the cessation or slowing down of the Cold War, how to deorganize the organization man if this seems desirable to do, and many others. The paper touches on the main points of the discussions that have been going on in the advisory groups and in the Seminar on the Corporation organized by Scott Buchanan. It does not pretend to be an *omnium gatherum* of problems about either the corporation or the economy. If there is any special theme in the paper, I would imagine it appears in Lincoln's words: "The dogmas of the quiet past are inadequate for the stormy present. We must think anew, we must act anew, we must disenthrall ourselves."

HUTCHINS: Anything that anybody wants to say on the subject of the economic order and its relation to freedom and justice is relevant.

NIEBUHR: It is just on that point I want to speak. I am always struck by the parallelism between the Corporation Project and the Trade Union Project. I think at some place or other in what we do as consultants and what is finally done, there must be some over-all consideration of this parallel, because they are so similar and the problems are so similar. If you take it in conjunction with the old liberalism and the kind of liberalism we are trying to elaborate, it is similar. We have a kind of new feudalism. The question is whether it is under control or whether it is self-controlled. There is also the question whether you can contain individual liberties in these new quasi-jurisdictions or sub-jurisdictions. The parallelisms ought to be brought out very clearly.

JACOBS: I think that is probably right. The problem is to try not to make too mechanical parallelisms. In terms of relating the union as a corporation to the corporation as a union, I think this would be interesting and productive to try.

NIEBUHR: Wouldn't the parallel between individual rights and these quasi-sovereignties be illuminating? Take the Kennedy labor bill in the Senate; on the whole, it is designed to preserve the individual rights of the workers as against the sovereignties of the big union bosses. The big bosses practically control the labor unions, which are almost identical with the Democratic Party. We have not a Labor Party but the liberal wing of the Democratic Party on the whole. There is a great deal of political power here, as there is in the corporations. It is a circular thing. Unions have their own power, and then they have the political power to determine how much control can be put on them or not.

JACOBS: I am not sure if that parallels anything in the corporation situation.

FERRY: It is one thing to say that the labor union and the corporation are related. That is obvious. It is tempting to consider that a real parallelism exists between the corporation and the union. I wish I were absolutely certain that this is a reasonable and real analogy. I am not sure that it is. Let me exemplify that with the so-called McClellan Bill of Rights, which went in and out of the labor bill. I did a little rewriting of those particular "Bill of Rights" sections and put in the word "corporation" where the words "labor union" appear. It seemed to me reasonable to inquire, at

29

least, whether if such a statute should be passed dealing with labor unions a similar statute enforcing similar standards on corporations should not be passed. Does that sound reasonable to you? I am not sure whether it sounds reasonable.

KERR: I would be in favor of the general idea. From all I have seen of this bill of rights in the newspaper accounts, I would agree with the general idea. The details might have to be changed.

HUTCHINS: Are you in favor of the bill of rights for unions, or are you for it for the corporations if the union has it?

KERR: No, for both of them. My own feeling is that it would be desirable to approach them together. To say there is a single problem is not to say you are anti-union or anti-corporation, but that there is a problem of individual rights to be concerned about in the corporation, trade union, and professional associations like the AMA and so forth. I favor the general idea very much.

MILLIS: The corporation bill of rights would not be the same.

KERR: It would not, and that is why I say the details would be different. The basic philosophy would be the same.

HOFFMAN: You are in favor of individual rights against the union so that the member is protected in his dissent if he wishes to make it, in his attempt to change the leadership, or to assail the leadership for its performance, access to the union, and the right to get out?

KERR: Not only against the leadership, but also against the majority.

HOFFMAN: So, thinking of the AMA, you would think that an individual doctor ought to be protected in his right to his dissent from the view of the professional association? His right to practice should not be endangered?

KERR: Yes.

HOFFMAN: Not to be penalized by it for any attitudes he has on matters outside of medicine?

KERR: Outside of medicine, yes. If it is malpractice, it is different. That would be like a person being a poor workman who might be kicked out of his craft.

HOFFMAN: But his politics, his religion, or his race ought not to affect his right to practice.

KERR: Yes. I might say that corporations have employees as unions have members.

MILLIS: The bill of rights would be guarantees to the individual employees.

KERR: As employees primarily, yes. There are some problems, however.

MILLIS: This is not true of the stockholder.

KERR: Not the stockholder. There may be some rights of the consumer which need to be protected, too. Equal access, for example. This is not so important for the ultimate consumer, but there are some intermediate stages where you can protect access of jobbers, and so forth.

MILLIS: The automobile dealers would be an example.

KERR: Yes, that type.

FERRY: It is not quite clear to me where the parallel grows close together and where it separates. I find a great deal of resistance on the part of corporations to the concept of a corporation as a private government.

On the other hand, they say, why, sure, a trade union is a private government. What else is it, if it is not a private government? What about the need for more democracy in unions? Those union fellows should govern themselves. But corporate spokesmen totally resist the notion that the corporation itself is also a private government, and has some of those attributes. Why is that?

NIEBUHR: That is the very significance. In *Business as Government* Beardsley Ruml spells out all these things. What you are dealing with is a quasi-sovereignty. The big labor boys draw their power from a quasi-democratic process, and the government tries to assure that this process will be purer than it has been. With the corporations you have stockholders. When Adolf Berle raises the question of the legitimacy of the corporation's authority, it is almost identical with the question about the legitimacy of the union's authority. They are different in actual power realities, but the moral problem is the same: Is there legitimacy?

FERRY: I have found that the best way to introduce the constitutional concept to people who speak for corporations is to ask them: "If the Constitution were being written today, something would be said in it, don't you think, about the labor union?"

"You're damned right," they answer. "It is a great center of power. There should be constitutional restraints and control."

This provides a very easy introduction to the question: "Would the Constitution also say something about the corporation?"

NIEBUHR: The recognition of the new sovereignty of labor came later than the recognition of the sovereignty of the corporation, not in the law but in the ethos of the culture. What health we have is due to the fact that these dubious sovereignties balance each other.

HUTCHINS: A paper that Robert Lekachman wrote for the Religion Project takes off from the proposition that in America we do not like people who have power. We are willing for them to have power but not too much. We don't care about the Protestants because we know that they are weak and disorganized. We don't have to pay any attention to them except when they get excited about things like Prohibition. We don't have to pay any attention to the Jews except when they get excited about things like Zionism, and start to monkey with our foreign policies. But "these Catholics" are getting more powerful all the time. That is why the church-state question is really a Catholic question.

By the same token, labor is always labor. It is always the labor movement. The picture is of a single unified group of people working hard toward clearly defined aims. I don't know how many thousands of corporations there are in the country. Nobody pays any attention to the NAM and the United States Chamber of Commerce. Even the president of General Motors can console himself by thinking that he is only one unit in only one business. But here are these labor boys in there working all the time "to take over the country."

NIEBUHR: On the whole there is a legitimacy in that. Madison argued in the *Federalist Papers* that the reason you had to have a federal government is that you had to have dispersion of centers of interest. The more you had them dispersed over a wide field, the safer you would be. In the present situation the obvious centralization of influence, interest, and power lies in the labor unions and the Catholic Church. They are the ones that are not dispersed enough.

HUTCHINS: Yet the fact of the matter is that organized labor is numerically declining, is it not, in proportion to the total work force?

JACOBS: Yes. There is a great illusion about the power of the labor movement, and it is going to get shattered as the new kind of union emerges. The pattern of the union in the future is going to be the Teamsters Union rather than the Automobile Workers Union; that is, a general amalgamated union closely comparable to what you have in England in the transport and general workers union or the general municipal workers. This is another reflection of the change in the American corporation that is taking place, and the breakdown of certain kinds of industry, and the building up of other industries. The fact that the union of the future will look like the Teamsters rather than the old Steelworkers is going to have a sharp effect on the political operations of the union, and also on the power of the union.

HOFFMAN: If you are going to talk about parallels between the labor movement and the corporation, you raise the question of the general ends of these two kinds of enterprises, and I don't think they are the same. The labor movement is a subsidiary institution in the sense that it is organized against the corporations or the employers. Its purpose is to get something out of them for the people they employ. What the labor movement has to offer or withhold is the time and energy of people. Corporations are organized for the disposition of property.

HUTCHINS: It has been suggested that perhaps the unions are going to disappear on the ground that whatever function they had is disappearing. This could not be suggested, I take it, about the industrial corporation. You may want to reform it or regulate it or change it, but you don't propose to abolish it. Yet you can seriously think about eventual elimination of unions?

JACOBS: Yes, I can conceive of this. The present function of the union could conceivably disappear. You might have the form of the union still existing, but it would be given a different purpose. For example, in some countries of the world today what is called a union has a quite different function from that of an American union. The union in a Communist country is simply an instrument to increase production. In colonial countries, the function of the union is not to quarrel with the employer over the disposition of the profits, but to teach people to work.

There is a big debate in the U.S. as to whether unions increase wages. My own feeling is that they do not. There is a whole school of economists who can demonstrate that wages would have risen without unions. The concept of the union which I take to be its real motivating drive is not wages, but something else entirely. It is the role the union plays in endowing the individual worker with a sense of respect for himself. If that function is taken away by some change in the attitude and in the function of corporations, I think unions would tend to wither away. There is already some evidence that this may be happening.

BUCHANAN: Some of the anomalies we are pointing out in the analogy here are due to the fact that the union is not a parallel organization. It is a part that is reflecting the whole. The union gets a kind of sovereignty because the corporation has a kind of sovereignty. If you separate them, it is like cutting a flat worm; you cut the body up, and it grows a head and a body but not a complete one. It is a dwarfed affair.

Supposing there was some connection as a part of the whole between the union and the corporation, I would like to ask Ferry if he would then want to go on with one of his main doctrines, that the corporation ought to be by charter restricted to profit-making.

FERRY: I don't accept the argument. Jacobs just explained that the union of the future is not going to be the union working in a plant, it is going to be on the pattern of the Teamsters. So the union, while it may be a part of a plant, will be very much more than a part of the corporation. At the same time it is a large social institution.

1785512

BUCHANAN: I am talking about a symbiosis between the union and the corporation. The union would not exist without a corporation and vice versa.

RABI: Do you conceive of the union's becoming something that sells labor to a corporation?

BUCHANAN: No. I am thinking about a highly structured corporation in which the union would be a part of the structure. It seems to me that when you drive the corporation back to its profit-only purpose, you are cutting out its vitality in connection with all the surrounding things but particularly in connection with the union.

NIEBUHR: What you say about the union's being within the structure of the corporation is refuted by Clark Kerr's analysis of the record in Germany, where they tried to coordinate the union into a corporation and thought they had made a great achievement in having union representation on the board of directors. Kerr said this did not work the way they expected it to, because these people became corporation officials and did not represent what was legitimate in the "class struggle."

HUTCHINS: You say the profit-making aim might prevent the development of the structure of the corporation as a social institution which might have to include the labor union in that structure. What it would have to include is labor, not the labor union. If you had the United States Steel Corporation organized on certain lines, it would certainly have to make some provision for the constitutionalization of labor within that corporation. But that need not necessarily be the United Steelworkers or any other organization. It might be organized under an analogy to a university faculty, which is not a national organization. The construction of a corporation according to Buchanan's ideals does not necessarily involve the maintenance of a national union of any kind. It might involve it, perhaps it should involve it, but it does not necessarily involve it.

GOLDMAN: You are assuming that Ferry is calling for taking the corporation back to a purely profit motive. Is that correct?

FERRY: I should like to see the corporation more erect, definable, less sprawling and undefined than it is now.

BUCHANAN: Ferry is standing for profit only very strongly. He thinks this is the only way you can make sense of the corporation. This seems to me very regressive.

HUTCHINS: Can we have an elaboration of the definition first before we go on to determine whether it is regressive or not? As I understand it, anything that the corporation could do that made it more profitable in the long run would be acceptable to Ferry?

BUCHANAN: I want to make a stronger point. The corporation was set up first as a mercantile arm of the government, and then it was set free, and then it was regulated; and this has ended in an anomalous situation. The business corporation is the only corporation that is set up for profit only. This sounds as if other corporations did not have income and circulation of capital, and the use of capital, labor, and a whole lot of things of this sort. They all have these economic functions. They have a social purpose.

The business corporation has been defined as an organization that has no purpose at all except to keep itself in operation. It may make some nice accidental contributions to society which Ferry calls public welfare. But, actually, profit is not a *purpose* of any corporation. It couldn't be. Profit, as I understand it now, even in the larger corporations in this country is a way of accumulating capital. It means dividends for the stockholders, but actually the main purpose of profit is to continue the organization. It is not an external purpose. This seems to me to make a very perverse organization, an organization that feeds itself, and then gets embarrassed because it can't find out what its social function is.

MURRAY: There would be two points of view. You could think of the people running the corporation as motivated only by the profit motive. That is what they want to do. That is their dynamism. It is quite a different question to determine what the objective end of the total enterprise is. I agree with you that you cannot say it is sheer profit. That may be the subjective motive of the people who manage it and hold executive positions and so on, but it cannot be the purpose of the thing itself. That must be specified in terms of some good of society as such.

HUTCHINS: Let us inquire as to the relation between the first proposition under the Argument, and what you have just said. The Argument refers to the economy and not to the corporation. The corporation is a principal agent within the economy.

BUCHANAN: This is a very radical proposition with which most economists don't agree. I don't take exception to it myself.

HUTCHINS: Then the question would be how Mr. Ferry fits No. 1 and his proposition about the corporation together.

FERRY: They fit very well together. The aims of society are not necessarily those of the corporation. I think a society can and should develop its own style. We live in a corporate style in this country. Perhaps that has been inevitable up to this point. This need not always be so. This is the reform that is suggested here. It is not suggested that the corporation ought to be eliminated. It need only be returned to its original function, which was a chartered function. The corporation was selected as the best means for carrying on certain activities in society. It was not expected at any point in our early history to set the style for the entire society. Proposition 1 says that the economy is a prominent and necessary part of society, but is not all of society. Later, the statement says that a bias in favor of the corporation as a profit-making institution will be observed throughout. It states that this instrumentality is necessary, and that the corporation is a fine thing to have around. However, it should not become the pervasive institution of our extra-government life. It should be used as an instrument of the general welfare. I regard the corporation as an instrument that is sprawling over too much of society now and imposing its own goals, which it cannot clearly comprehend, on the rest of the community.

GOLDMAN: I did not get the impression that you wanted to get the corporation back to a sheer profit motive. I would object simply to the impracticality of your suggestion. I think you misread the corporation. When it was first started in this country, it was not simply a profit-making thing. You were supposed to make money from it, but the canals and turnpikes were supposed to serve the public. The corporation, as you say, has been constantly expanding, with constantly expanding functions. You are asking for something which may or may not be correct but which is impossible under the present circumstances. I would rather see the argument go: Let us find out what the corporation does, let us try to make its functions clear and compact, let us perhaps lop off this and that in the charter, but let us assume that it is going to be something more than a profit-making instrument, as it always has been.

NIEBUHR: What you say about the economy is quite obviously right. Then you say, but the corporation must be clearly defined as a profit-making institution. You have a parallel of that in the modern Communist oligarchy. The original motive of the Communist oligarchy was to produce revolution. But that is not what the Communist oligarchy is doing today. You cannot confine it to its original purpose as you can't confine the corporation to its original purpose. The Vanderbilts wanted to make money through the railroads, but we allowed it for the sake of opening the West.

FERRY: Perhaps, instead of "return to a profit-making role," one should say "advance to a profit-making role" out of the welter of social welfare activities in which corporations are now engaged.

RABI: I am confused with such different functions. Take the AT&T corporation, which has a fairly well-defined function. Certainly you cannot say it is a profit-making organization, although it makes profit. It would not exist if it did not give the public service. Then you have other corporations—let us say the various corporations in the paper industry—which are competing with one another. AT&T is hardly competing. It is giving service and getting a return. Then you have organizations which are large holding companies. They have a great variety of industry. Then again you come to something else like IBM, which utilizes whatever money it makes to do more of the same thing. I don't understand how you put this under one general aim and how you are going to discuss this as "the corporation."

FERRY: I recognize, of course, the variety of corporations, large and small, with differing outlooks. When I say I have a bias in favor of profit-making as the standard or the rationale for corporate activity, I mean to say that I cannot see anything else that is as reasonable. The first part of the paper is given to the argument that there is no satisfactory rationale for corporate activity today. You suggest that there may be a great many different rationales and theories. Perhaps this is the case. Edward S. Mason pointed out that Adam Smith and the classical economists, during all of the Nineteenth Century while American capitalism was growing, provided a perfectly satisfactory explanation of what they were doing and why they were doing it. He says that no such apologia is now present and it is more needed than anything else in American economic life because without it nothing is comprehensible. I do not say that an advance to profit-making will solve all problems. I propose profit-making because it is to me the only intelligible standard for corporate activity.

MURRAY: Why do you want to make it so very intelligible? The trouble is that all the classical theories that were so frightfully intelligible—Marxism on the one side and classical liberalism on the other—were perhaps for that very reason dated, transitory, destined to disappear, with all their false clarity shattered. Mind you, I am not against intelligibility.

HUTCHINS: You would be for true clarity.

MURRAY: Like Aristotle, as far as the nature of the material permits.

HUTCHINS: There is no standard at present by which to measure the performance of a corporation. I think this is going to cause serious economic and political problems.

MURRAY: Must you have a single standard?

HUTCHINS: I don't know that the standard has to be the same for every type of corporation. In fact, one of Carl Kaysen's suggestions is that you might have a different general regulation or lack of regulation for different types or sizes of corporations. I think that is worth considering.

NIEBUHR: I would like to elaborate on Murray's remarks that you can't have too simple a theory, and that there is no advantage in saying the corporation must get back or go forward to a simple theory of profit-making. Let us say that the classical theory was right that the society harnessed motives that were not in over-all terms good. Adam Smith said we don't engage in benevolence but in self-regard. It is significant that the whole classical economy, which regarded profit as a primary motive, was wrong in its simplicity. It was wrong even about the people themselves and what their real motives were. I mention the two motives that classical economy left out—power and, something more positive, creativity.

If you take the history of the Ford Motor Company, you realize how complex this is. Henry Ford the first explicitly defied the classical theory and said that owners were supposed to be engaged in profit-seeking, but he was not. He had only two motives. One was to turn out human beings rather than cars, which was a fantastic bit of self-delusion, and the second was to raise the American economy. But, as I watched him in my younger days, I knew that his real motive was power. He used the workers terribly as against General Motors, which was more humanitarian but less pretentious about it. He had a mixture of motives. He did not understand his own motives. Yet on the whole it worked out. Then we have Henry Ford the second. What is his motive? The Ford Foundation siphons off most of the Ford Motor Company profits. Like the IBM, it is being run for its own purposes. In other words, these corporations do some of the things society says should be done, and that is not bad. So you have the IBM and the Bell Telephone Company and the Ford Motor Company. You can't take them back and say they must deal only with profits.

FERRY: The paper merely says that I have a bias in favor of the corporation as a profit-making institution. I have no simple-minded notion that it would be possible to transform the corporation into a profit-making institution solely and simply. I do, however, believe that it would be a great advantage not to accept the notion that because society has become more complicated, therefore it is perhaps not possible or even desirable to have a more rational understanding of the role of the corporation in society. I am struck by statements of the management of Standard Oil of New Jersey and others that the role of management today is that of a steward taking care of the several interests of the corporation—those of the stockholders, those of the employees, those of the consumers, those of the general welfare. This concept of stewardship is ten or twelve years old now. The whole point of the paper is the distribution and use of corporate power. Do I understand you to say that this power can be trusted as it stands because of a growing concept of stewardship?

NIEBUHR: No, I am not as naïve as that. I may have accused you of naïveté. I am simply saying that whatever is bad in the corporation's use of power can't be corrected by saying it must go back to the original profit-making motive. It is a center of power. Perhaps the society should say the corporation should not have the right to practice benevolence, because it takes away from the stockholder the right to practice his own benevolence. So you have to put restraint upon its power in every way. The problem is the restraint upon its power, and not the problem of motive or getting back to the original motive.

MURRAY: I think this question of motives simply gets us into a blind alley. A man might be motivated to seek political office by reasons of personal ambition, not to make money, but frankly to gain the power. He becomes, let us say, a Senator, a Secretary of State, or what not. But when you finish talking about his motives, the office that he holds has a purpose quite apart from any motives that he has in seeking the office or administering it. Similarly here, I should not object to any businessman saying, "I am not in business for my health. I am in business to make money." That is not necessarily the purpose of his business. Maybe it is why I do what I do, but *what* I do has a purpose and end independently of *why* I do it.

American society is terribly preoccupied with motive. One of our disastrous things is the psychological order assuming primacy over the ontological order. Men are very conscious of their motives, and they don't like to stand in front of the public and say the economic order has a relative autonomy of its own. Prosperity is its purpose only publicly. All around is this vague idea that I must somehow be doing good. I must be helping people. I must try to make people happy. This subjective motivation is thrust into the objective operation with the results that you describe, namely, confusion.

When you sit down and look at what goes on, you would say this is just a lot of nonsense. You are not a humanitarian at all. You are a man in quest of power. It is all right for your speech-writer to put this stuff down, because this is the image that you must cast up to the public, because the social conscience nowadays requires it. Let us stop talking about people's motives. I don't care what people's motives are. I want to know what they are doing and what the effects are, and which ones are good and which ones are bad. I don't care why you hold this office or why you run this business. It will always be true, I should think, that people will go into business to make money. What is wrong with that?

BUCHANAN: You would want to talk about purpose as distinguished from motive.

MURRAY: Purpose or end. If I were to use my own terminology, I would use end.

BUCHANAN: The rest of the paper is concerned with the government's stating the purposes. In other words, Ferry is taking away the sense of purpose from the corporation and allowing it to be used explicitly and officially by the government. Am I right here, or am I overstating it?

FERRY: A bit overstated, but go ahead.

BUCHANAN: Why this division? Why do you leave the minimum of profit to the corporation and then load more on the government than at the moment it is able to take on? You are saying that our economic system has to know what its purpose is more than ever before. The machinery for doing this begins with the critical group you recommend but finally rises to a planning section of the government. Is that right?

FERRY: Yes. But it is premature to raise the question of planning, and especially in these terms. Planning as proposed later in the paper is not on quite as spectacular a scale as you suggest.

BUCHANAN: I am overstating it.

RABI: Corporations which have been organized for one thing have turned into quite different things. As an example, the Atomic Energy Commission, which has spent a lot of money, has no plants of its own. It does not operate anything. It is just a lot of men in Washington who give out money. The rest is done by corporations in one way or another. The University of California runs the two weapons development places, Livermore and Los Alamos. The University of Chicago runs the Argonne. Union Carbide runs Oak Ridge. These are examples of corporate forms at work. Then there are Defense Department orders for the manufacture of various things. The profits, if any, are subject to renegotiation. Here we have corporations specifically designed to go to the government. There must be thousands of them, ready to get contracts to do a piece of research or a piece of development. Why doesn't government do it itself? Because it found that this system is more flexible.

To use one word, corporation, is trying to deduce a simplification which won't be helpful. You could take one form of corporation, as you find it, and say it would be useful to explore a particular idea to a particular degree. For convenience, the tax laws ignore these various corporate purposes except for the nonprofit institutions. This might give us a kind of focus. But you have to make a whole lot of headings.

BUCHANAN: Shouldn't you recall that the term "corporation" here, and all the terms that go with it, are written into our law very elaborately? We did not make up this general term to cover all these diverse activities. The law did this a long time ago. It is continually articulating it, making all the distinctions you are talking about.

FERRY: I am quite aware of the enormous variety of corporations and the difficulties of an argument which would seem to cover IBM as well as Livermore and AT&T, Standard Oil and Ford Motor Company, to say nothing of hundreds of thousands of others. However, this was intentional. I hoped that this discussion would produce some suggestions of the kind that you have just made—that discrimination among certain classes and kinds of corporate activities is necessary. We made discriminations in setting up public utilities at one point. We separated off the railroads at another point and said special considerations of the public welfare require us to separate out the railroads and make them accountable. Now we come to a point where it may be necessary to make some further discriminations.

COGLEY: Isn't it a perfectly possible proposition that the corporation exists for the sake of profit? Specific corporations may have a specific end—a private end—as opposed to this general end. Isn't that an arguable proposition having nothing to do with motive at all?

Suppose I say the role of this corporation is profit-making. Then you might ask, what is the role of X company? You say it exists to make electricity. A manufacturer of ties makes ties. What we have to talk about is not the specific corporations and how their private ends are related to social ends, but what is the general role of the genus corporation in our society.

MURRAY: I fully agree, surely. Some are wealth-producing, some are wealth-distributing. I suppose you may even include Madison Avenue—the talkers. I don't think there is any reason why, despite the variety, they could not all be subsumed under some generic purpose. If I had to state it, I would say it is the public prosperity. It is the purpose of that particular order in society which we call the economy.

HUTCHINS: Would you find any distinction between what you have just said and Proposition No. 1 in the Argument?

MURRAY: No, though I would rephrase Proposition No. 1. It made me a little worried whether Ferry was trying to drive too sharp a distinction between this particular order of society and the political order, the cultural order, the various other orders that might be distinguished. This is an identifiable order within society which has, as such, a finality proper to itself. It has classically been defined as the public prosperity. It is defined in the first instance in material terms. This I think is where you are on good ground in talking about profits. This is a material concept. I should wish the primary objective of the economic order to be thus defined in material terms as I would not want the order of culture to be determined in material terms.

NIEBUHR: Rabi made the significant statement that the Atomic Energy Commission had all these contracts with corporations. For what purpose? To insure flexibility. I think that this contrast be-tween over-all guidance and planning and flexibility — flexibility meaning the engaging of various motives on lower levels and various lower centers of power—is more important than specula-tion about motives. What you face in a technical society ultimately —particularly America vis-à-vis Russia—is whether you are going to organize the over-all planning through a bureaucracy. Bureauc-racies are inefficient. Past a certain point they are certainly in-efficient.

Or are you going to have the classical liberal society concept: various centers of power with various centers of initiative? That, I think, is the ultimate problem that we face in the economic order. You can't solve that simply by talking about the economy, because we are dealing with something more. We are dealing with centers of power and centers of initiative all along the line.

GOLDMAN: Ferry has got into this trouble about motives because what he is looking for is a theory of the corporation without first looking for a theory of society. I would like to give two instances to clarify what I mean. In the last fifty or sixty years two important things have been going on in our society. One is that we have been deciding that more things ought to be done. For example, in 1900, as a people we did not believe that school-children who could not pay for milk at lunch should be provided with it. Now we have decided they should be given it.

The other change is a shift not in the theory of what should be done, but in who should do it. In 1900, for example, the assump-tion was that private colleges should be supported strictly by pri-vate benefactors. Now the assumption is that the corporation has some responsibility for such support. I don't think we can talk about a theory of the corporation that will get us any place without setting up first a theory of the good society, in which we decide in general what should be done. Then you would have to swivel your power centers as to who should do it. We would get some rather clear definitions of what the corporation should do if we went about it that way.

NIEBUHR: Wouldn't your theory of society say that a society must have some control over the purposes of the community? It is not restricted to purely material welfare, even in the economic sphere.

GOLDMAN: On what criterion would I decide whether children should or should not have free milk or whether they should or should not have milk, free or not? We don't have the purposes defined among ourselves.

HOFFMAN: One of the criteria is whether there is a lot of milk around that the government is stuck with and does not know what to do with.

GOLDMAN: That is not an over-all purpose.

MURRAY: That is the way things get done. That is part of the irrationality.

HOFFMAN: There were references earlier to the economic indeterminacy of these processes, our incapacity to make them simple and have a nice single unifying theory. Isn't this the sort of thing you are talking about—the surplus milk?

GOLDMAN: If you are going to answer the question whether the corporation should have anything to do with providing certain services, like education, or the government should have anything to do with providing other services, like milk for children, the first thing you have to decide is certain over-all purposes which will tell you whether to have the education to begin with or the milk to begin with. I don't think this argument of whether you have the milk around is pertinent to the setting up of these over-all goals.

MURRAY: You are probably right, but nonetheless you have the Topsy kind of thing. Take your second question, who does this? If I am not mistaken, the free lunch program for children is administered by the Department of Agriculture.

GOLDMAN: We decided that the government should do it in that case.

47

MURRAY: Why the Department of Agriculture? It is only because they have a surplus. First we had the milk. Then we decided what to do with the milk.

HUTCHINS: This happened in the case of corporate assistance to colleges and universities. The corporations should supply the money to the colleges and universities because the corporations were going to have the money. Nobody else would have it.

GOLDMAN: The thing that struck me in the decision opening up corporate giving to colleges was that the court had been provided with no philosophy of society on which to justify its decision. It ended up justifying the decision on the somewhat spurious ground that giving the money was in the self-interest of the corporations because the universities teach free enterprise.

HUTCHINS: Would it follow that, since education and support of higher learning are aims of the American people, the corporation should be free to support it and conduct it and deduct it as a business expense or as a charitable gift?

MURRAY: Suppose for the argument I said that the ultimate reason why corporations should contribute to private colleges is the brutal and bloody fact that they have the money, period. Suppose I say this is the end of the line, I will not theorize further.

FERRY: Since they have the money, they can give it. They can also withhold it. They can decide, to a degree, something about the character of private education by the act of giving or withholding.

HUTCHINS: If the support of a corporation or corporations can make or break a college, this has something to do with the college's autonomy and control over its content. The question may become: "Can the thing exist?"

RABI: Granting the corporation the right to give money does nothing else in my mind except to increase the power of the corporation. I see no particular quality of a corporation which makes it a judge of education. It is a fundamental mistake to ask corporations to do this. Furthermore, they have not got the money.

HUTCHINS: The object of colleges and universities in supporting the decision of the Smith case is the same as the object of the government in setting up the corporation income tax. The tax is wholly irrational, but it is a great convenience to the tax collector. So it is with the money collector for the university. Instead of having to appeal to 150,000,000 people, he can deal with the rich corporations.

RABI: In most of the discussions we have had, we have been talking about the large corporations. We are not talking about the half million little corporations. When we talk about the labor unions we are talking about the large labor unions. How many corporations are we talking about, about 200?

FERRY: These comments refer, let us say, to the 500 largest industrial corporations in the country.

RABI: If you left off the last 300, you would still be including most of them.

FERRY: Yes, but there are two important points. The first is that these corporations, while small in number, still control well over two-thirds of the industrial capacity. Second, they are the style-setters for the rest of industrial society. It seems to me appropriate to talk about them in this sense.

HUTCHINS: I wonder if we have done justice to Goldman's point. He is saying that we can't talk about the theory of the corporation and the theory of the economy presumably until we have a theory of society. We may be proceeding backwards; in fact, we may have been all the way through this enterprise. We may have decided to continue a kind of running discussion of the theory of society. At the same time we may be trying to develop theories of the mass media, corporation, labor union, and so on. These are concurrent enterprises. There is here an implicit theory of society as there is an express theory of the economic order.

NIEBUHR: I think there is an explicit theory underlying the work of this group. This theory is that we are trying, on the one hand, to assure the over-all purposes and ends of a good society, which would be material welfare, the general defense, culture, and so on, and, on the other hand, what Rabi calls flexibility, the vitality of the different parts.

In a democratic society we try to prevent the harmony of the whole from destroying the vitality of the parts. The philosophy, as I understand it, of our whole procedure is to grant that there is not going to be individual vitality in the sense that the old liberalism stood for, but that we will have collective vitalities of various kinds.

Rabi says it is not just the big corporation, not just the big labor union. No, it is not only that. We do have the problem of bigness. But we always have these collective centers of creativity. What we are trying to do is always to effect a balance, to link the flexibility of a free society and the spontaneity of centers of power with the over-all purposes. We still have the problem of guaranteeing the rights of the individual against centers of power. Perhaps we have two great problems—how to guarantee the rights of the individual against the centers of power, and, on the other hand, how to guarantee the vitalities of the centers of power, influence, creativity against bureaucracy, if you will.

MURRAY: There is more to it than the preservation of sheer spontaneity, whether individual or collective. It is something beyond these. What are these things spontaneous for? This problem came up in the liberal era, too. There was a general recognition that some things were as spontaneous as all get-out. They were spontaneous in a number of different wrong directions.

NIEBUHR: Yes. It is only the purpose of government to see to it that the over-all purposes are fulfilled within the terms of the spontaneous desires, motives, et cetera, of all the centers of power. This is the new liberalism as against the old liberalism. The old liberalism assumed that spontaneity, free enterprise, free market, all contributed to the general welfare. We know that is not true.

We know there must be checks and balances. The government, if it finds one center of power too strong, must raise up another center of power in the interest of justice.

MURRAY: We are also finding out, perhaps, that the great advantage of the large organization, which is I presume efficiency, may not be or perhaps should not be the controlling value. That is to say, in order to get more and more efficiency, we would therefore get more and more bigness. Maybe there should be a point where some other value comes in to assume the primacy over sheer efficiency of operation in the name of something higher.

NIEBUHR: How would you define the higher value? Liberty, flexibility, spontaneity, wouldn't you?

MURRAY: I suppose in terms of the adjective "good" in the good society, whatever specific meaning one might attach to that word in different contexts. For instance, you might say that the cult of efficiency resulting in the cult of bigness does not make for the goodness of society. Then I would have to say what I meant in a particular case by goodness. I might show the cult of bigness impinging on the political order and damaging the political good. It might impinge on the individual order and damage the individual good. It might impinge on the cultural and spiritual order by excessive emphasis on sheer material values. I would have then to specify what good was being damaged in any particular case.

NIEBUHR: If you specify goodness in terms of society, you will always come to two regulated principles, and regulated only because they are not absolutely realizable. They are liberty and equality. They are not absolute forms. They can't be because either absolute liberty or absolute equality would destroy a society.

MURRAY: They are probably too exclusively political norms, unless you are willing to extend them in economic and cultural directions.

NIEBUHR: Yes, you have to extend them in all directions. What is wrong about the segregated schools? Violation of equal justice.

Equality before the law, equality of opportunity, and so forth. That goes beyond the political order. That goes to the cultural sphere.

GOLDMAN: Don't we have to push the question about the theory of society a little further; that is, how does a good society operate in general? The normative principles are what we want to get to. Running through our discussion is an unanswered question. Does the good society operate by telling each power center what its function is; that is, we say to a corporation, you are supposed to do so and so. Or does the good society operate by letting its power centers move in wherever there is a vacuum, wherever people want something done? A corporation moves in. The government moves in. The Department of Agriculture moves in. Or whatever it may be. I think we must decide this before we can talk about what the corporation ought to do.

NIEBUHR: I agree with you. The ultimate question is: Shall these power centers fill in vacuums as they appear, or should the over-all planning agency, government and so forth, decide how far to go or not to go? If you ask it in the second way, you have collectivism. If you answer in the first way, you have free enterprise. Obviously we are striving for something in between. I don't think Ferry's statement has the in-between sufficiently clear, because there is at least a suggestion that society must guarantee the over-all goals and tell the centers of power what is and what is not their business. What we are after is a *modus vivendi* between the old free enterprise and the old collectivism.

GOLDMAN: Is it correct that your paper is posited on in-between theories?

FERRY: It is intended to be so posited. At one end stands the conviction that the corporation is a means and not an end of society. It is just one of many means toward the good society, however defined. With this goes the statement that the society, acting through government, can set the limits of corporate activity and can exact certain performance.

MURRAY: Would you accept this qualification to that last proposition? It can only set limits if there previously have been identified encroachments of some sort or another on a good which society wants protected.

GOLDMAN: I don't quite see how we make the application of the general principle to the specific case. How does that in-between principle answer the question about the need for money for private colleges? Who moves in there?

MURRAY: I think that this is both in fact and perhaps maybe in good theory settled on purely empirical grounds.

GOLDMAN: On the grounds of who has the money?

MURRAY: After somebody has moved in, then a problem may arise which would require reconciliation. There are guardians of the republic somewhere around, presumably. Or were you suggesting that there should be some *a priori* decisions made in this matter as to who moves in where and how far?

GOLDMAN: Don't we need it? Or else it is not in-between principle.

MURRAY: In what concerns means toward ends I am as willing to be as pragmatist as anybody in sight. That is no argument against it.

NIEBUHR: I question the sheer pragmatism. Yet I agree that if you have defined ends, which are partly contradictory and partly complementary, then the way you fulfill them must be purely empirical according to historic contingency.

GOLDMAN: Then does Ferry have any basis to criticize the fact that the corporations are giving money to the colleges? In the jostling process they have got in. Public opinion and ten thousand other things have caused this.

NIEBUHR: The only way you can criticize it is if you can point out that it has disturbed some real good. In the educational process, for instance, someone suggests that there is an overweight of corporation support for the sciences as against the humanities or something like that. But these are all empirical tests that you have to apply.

Hutchins: What I want to find out is in what sense you mean pragmatic and whether there is no other standard than the palpable standard of success. For example, when it is said that the college has to have autonomy, this implies a standard that is derived from a conception of the purpose of this institution. I could say, *a priori*, that I have very serious questions about corporate giving because the purpose of an educational institution may not be achieved if the United States Steel Corporation helps to decide whether or not it should be carried out.

By the same token, if there is a purpose of a corporation and if it is to make profits, then the fact that it can spend its money or can get away with giving its money to philanthropy would not affect me very much. I would say only that this institution is being used for purposes for which it was not created.

My understanding is that there are two questions here. One is whether government will determine, does determine, must determine, what goods and services are required by society. The other question is, what are goods and services and what is the economy? The first seems to have some light shed on it by Proposition No. 5, which says: "Society has the power and authority to state the ends and conditions that are to be met by the economy." It does not say that society will exercise this power or authority. It says it possesses it.

Buchanan: This is not clear to me or self-evident. I think that people are saying no, this has never been the American assumption, and it is not now. But I agree with the radical statement.

Niebuhr: Could I ask whether many of these questions are not concerned with the concept "economic ends"? The economy is subsidiary to society, which has ends in addition to its economic ends. These economic ends are in the whole context of what society wants. If you say economic ends, you are inclined to make material well-being a sort of absolute, which it is not. Perhaps what you ought to say is that the economy is subsidiary to society which must use economic means for its various ends, general defense, common welfare, and so on.

HUTCHINS: I would agree with that formulation.

MURRAY: Are you suggesting, Buchanan, that people would react to Proposition No. 1 in the Argument as radical? They would instantly attach to it a socialist meaning?

BUCHANAN: Collectivist; not any particular brand of socialism. It is saying that society in some sense is a system which does control all economic activities.

MURRAY: That implication is certainly not necessary in Ferry's proposition. Maybe you can read it in. You can read half a dozen economic systems into Proposition No. 1.

HUTCHINS: Do you find the implication in Proposition 5?

MURRAY: No. I am not saying who is allocating. I say these two things must somehow be allocated in terms of the general welfare. The next question is, who is going to do the allocating or is it to be left to "bumps and grinds"? Maybe the word "allocation" is bad.

HUTCHINS: You are using "allocation" in a certain specific historical sense.

BUCHANAN: I had a conversation about a week ago with a Britisher who was asking what the Fund was doing, and I said that one of the problems is that we could not find any economist who could describe to us what our economic system is. He said, "What makes you think you have one?" He said there is no reason why anyone should suppose that this kind of activity that is mentioned here has any given purpose. It just happens. That is what I have in the back of my mind here.

RABI: That thought was behind my questions, too.

GOLDMAN: It seems to me that Father Murray requires the economy to sustain personal dignity, which means that the economy of the U.S. is not operating that way for about 150,000,000 people.

MURRAY: Yes. I want to make public prosperity an ethical requirement.

NIEBUHR: May I ask if this argument does not show that we left out at least at the beginning the very great question about government and the people? If you leave that out, it might sound like Fidel Castro's "the people": "What the people want, we want."

FERRY: The way I think the Argument might best be considered is as a series of dicta that might appear in a Supreme Court decision on a case concerning the proper role of General Electric, let us say. The Argument is supposed to underscore and explain certain of the proposals that follow. It goes much further than the proposals in some respects and falls short in others.

HUTCHINS: How would you interpret, Father Murray, the first sentence of Proposition 7 in this context?

MURRAY: If you don't read into this any ideology, I don't fall on my face over it. It has a beautiful vagueness. I don't have much trouble with the first sentence. My difficulty begins with the second one: "This includes formal planning." This is too dogmatic, unless Ferry is supposing that we are living in a particular set of circumstances.

HUTCHINS: That is the way I would interpret it. "Whatever mechanisms and controls" is certainly as broad as you can get. These are the first four words of the sentence. Then you say this may even include under certain circumstances formal planning by the national government.

GOLDMAN: Isn't Buchanan's point really not so much what these words are saying, but the connotations that have come to be attached to them in some circles in the United States?

BUCHANAN: They do not merely not represent the consensus, but they have been sharply objected to by certain people.

FERRY: I think it might be useful to read exactly what Dean Courtney Brown of the Columbia School of Business has to say. His is the voice, so to speak, of non-acceptance. "This fairly formidable array of statements rests basically on the premise that government is a more reliable custodian of public welfare than privately assigned individuals and institutions; that the correspondence between long-run profitability of a corporation and its esteem with the public is either unknown to management or that they are uninterested, and that the values of a pluralist society with foci of power scattered throughout is of limited significance, and that the concept of voluntarism may have outworn much of its usefulness."

MURRAY: Do you accept this as a statement of your postulates?

FERRY: No, but this is the way he reads them.

HUTCHINS: Let me summarize where we are. We discussed the parallels and differences between corporations and labor unions, and got into a discussion of profit-making as the aim of the corporation. It was felt that this was too simple, too general, did not represent the true motives of operators of corporations in so far as motives were relevant at all.

We then, at Goldman's instigation, got into the question of the relationship between a theory of a corporation and a theory of society. In this it became apparent that what we were after was something intermediate between having the government tell the power centers what they ought to do and a theory of "bumps and grinds."

We then discussed with more or less depth Propositions Nos. 1, 2, 5, and 7, in the Argument. Now we are ready to come to the question, if you wish to, what do you yourselves think about the economic order and the corporation?

MURRAY: I would like to say this in favor and praise of what I take to be a basic postulate underlying this whole paper, namely, the primacy of the political. I am all for that. Admittedly, it is a difficult principle to apply. It needs to be recalled today and given meaning in terms of the existing situation.

NIEBUHR: I think that is a good way of putting it. The paper says quite truly that the economy must be subject to society. The question is whether in our kind of liberal society we have not put the cart before the horse and whether we are not the first society that has operated for the economy. Consider the luxury standards and other things we maintain for the sake of keeping the machine going. There is where the means become an end. Certainly it has disturbed the primacy of the political. Not that the political is more moral than the economic, but the political contains the conscious designs of a society more than the economic, which operates by instinctive process or whatever. We are looking for the primacy of the political without authoritarianism and without getting into the authoritarian society.

RABI: I wish I knew what it meant when you say the primacy of the political. Do you mean explicit political aims in the ordering of the social structure, or do you mean a particular class of people, or what?

MURRAY: I mean quite concretely the right and duty of government, representing the political order, to play a role in the economy and a role superior to the forces that operate within the economy. It is my impression that the pattern of interference between the political and economic as exhibited in America has largely been the government coming down into the economic order as another economic force.

RABI: No. The anti-trust laws are not an economic force. It is a definite ordering. The surplus profit taxes, the taxation system, are definite orderings. The development of an economic force in some of the instances I gave earlier is still something else. It is a matter of efficiency, the political not being able to solve the problem of making an efficient operation, particularly an efficient industrial operation, and resorting to other schemes to get around its own political difficulties. For that reason I don't really know what you meant by your reaffirming the supremacy of the political. It has been there all the time. Why didn't they like Roosevelt? He was using the political power. They didn't like the other Roosevelt either.

HUTCHINS: It was Coolidge who said that the business of America was business. I would say the tone of the present administration is the same.

RABI: If you are talking about a particular administration, that is something else.

HUTCHINS: I think that is the tradition of the United States since the Civil War. I suggest that the American ideal is "bumps and grinds," and that every time it is necessary for the government to intervene to ease the effects of bumps and grinds, there have to be the deepest apologies to everybody, and the greatest possible concealment of what is going on.

RABI: Aren't you glad about what is going on? If you had complete government control in a country like the United States without a system of selection as in a country like Russia, we would be run by incompetents.

BUCHANAN: What about adequate control?

RABI: If it means getting a level of subsistence, that is another matter.

BUCHANAN: What I think would be adequate political control of this society would be thought by most people to be taking over everything.

NIEBUHR: You don't mean by primacy that the *sole* power must be political. You can distinguish between the political and economic orders and say the political order operates in terms of explicit purposes. This is what we think is good for society. The economic order obviously operates implicitly. Classical economy says people seeking their own ends will serve the good of society. This has proved to be inadequate. Rabi is right in saying you have to allow for some of this. For one thing, there is no bureaucrat who knows enough. So you have to have a *modus vivendi.* You have to have the primacy of the political, but you must not rule out these implicit harmonies that develop on their own level.

BUCHANAN: Is the economy to serve society?

NIEBUHR: Ultimately, yes. But maybe the bureaucrat does not know as well what society requires as the society itself finds out, in the way Goldman suggests.

BUCHANAN: But suppose the agents of the economy discover what they think is their interest and what they think is society's interest. This is what the corporation is trying to do at present, or thinks it is doing. What should happen if the corporation discovered what the economy was for? Suppose they could state their purposes and those of the economy objectively, who should have the responsibility, the government or the corporations?

NIEBUHR: Both.

BUCHANAN: Yes, but in what relation? If you mean primacy of the political, don't you mean that the government has an essential job of recognizing, chartering, regulating, and so forth? I am not necessarily saying operating or controlling. You have to have the political judgment recognized as primary, if you mean the primacy of the political.

NIEBUHR: The primacy of the political would mean that society, operating through its explicit controls and its explicitly stated purposes, reserves to itself the right to say whether these automatic policies work or not. For instance, if the automatic processes don't work except on the obvious goods and services level, and don't work for the common defense, general welfare, et cetera, society does what it has in fact already done. This is why we have not complete but only some primacy of the political.

MURRAY: Maybe the word "primacy" is a little bit of a trap. By using it, I am not saying that government presides or possesses the initiative in regard to the whole economic order. Perhaps the better word almost might be the ultimacy of the political. I would wish to have any political control and regulation of the economy done only in the instance of need, demonstrable and demonstrated.

HOFFMAN: The last resort.

MURRAY: Yes. Not the government standing at the beginning and saying, "This is the way it will be." It rather stands above and chiefly says, "This is the way it will *not* be."

HUTCHINS: The classical statement that politics is the architectonic science does not mean that the political order everywhere impinges in every detail on the other orders in society. When Aristotle used the phrase, he was applying it to education. He was not taking the position that the state was going to run education in every detail. The aims of the state necessarily determine—this is Goldman's position—what goes on within the state. The fact that politics is the architectonic science doesn't mean that the state is going to intervene at every point in the operation of the economic order. This is a matter of judgment as to time, circumstance, and necessity. Is any more than that meant when you talk about the primacy of the political?

MURRAY: No. My remark was largely prompted by what I considered to be Mr. Brown's gross misunderstanding both of the tenor of Ferry's paper and also of the way things ought to be. He says the paper rests basically on the premise that government is a more reliable custodian of public welfare than privately assigned individuals or institutions. This is a completely irrelevant and meaningless statement. Nobody is saying this at all. Least of all am I saying it when I say primacy of the political. It doesn't mean government is a better custodian of anything. Government is a necessary control and regulating principle just as law itself is. In the ultimate instance, it assumes the right to say this is the way it will be, and chiefly this is the way it will not be.

HUTCHINS: I would be interested to know the meaning of the words "privately assigned." Does he mean accidentally assigned?

MURRAY: I suppose so.

BUCHANAN: He means corporation executives.

HUTCHINS: No. I think he means assignments that have been arrived at through non-governmental action; that is, through the operation of anonymous pressures in the society.

BUCHANAN: But pretty much through corporation activity. It seems to me that the proposition that he is attributing to Ferry is correctly attributed in the first place, and that it is true, isn't it? You are saying, no, it isn't true, and I don't understand what you think it is. It seems to me you are saying the same thing Brown is.

MURRAY: Maybe it is the word "reliable" that gags me. If Brown says that the government is the custodian, I couldn't agree more. The question of the reliability of who is to do something best is what I mean by an irrelevance, except in the pragmatic order after we have tried a number of ways of running the railroads, and we find that this has to be a public utility.

BUCHANAN: Brown is saying that government is unreliable, that you cannot depend upon it to do that job.

MURRAY: I would not rely on the government to do any economic job in the first instance.

BUCHANAN: Then what do you mean by what you are saying? If government is a custodian of the public welfare, it must have some duties of an economic nature.

MURRAY: They are basically discharged through the instrumentality of law or what would be equivalent to the law.

BUCHANAN: You say that is not doing anything economic? If it makes regulations governing corporations and labor unions and so on?

MURRAY: It is exercising a political function.

BUCHANAN: But it has an incidence in controlling the economy.

MURRAY: Very much.

GOLDMAN: As our discussion goes on, I am confused by one thing. Ferry, in the Argument are you stating what is or what ought to be?

FERRY: The Argument says, here are the general ideas on which the following material is based. The Argument is not intended to be an outline or historical or contemporary account of the way things are. It describes in rather a formal way what seems to me to be the current situation, and it hinges really on Father Murray's useful phrase, the primacy of the political.

GOLDMAN: We don't know what general welfare means. Dean Brown would say that the general welfare of the United States is most involved in keeping a free country. A free country is a country in which individuals have initiative, et cetera, et cetera. In this way you get back to an anti-primacy of politics argument. If this is the way you define general welfare, he is right. On the other hand, I assume Ferry is defining the general welfare in what might be called a more New Dealish or more liberal sense.

MURRAY: By general welfare the implication in the Argument is that in addition to economic ends there are other ends, and the service of all these ends in their organic relationship constitutes what you mean by the general welfare, including what would be a political end. The first proposition in the Argument distinguishes the economy as a particular order in society. The second says the economy is not the only order within society. In fact, it is not the highest order within society, but is an order subservient to a whole that is larger than itself. The Argument assigns to this economic order in society the purpose of production and distribution of material goods and services.

HUTCHINS: I assume that Proposition 3, for example, simply means that the society has other ends than the economic ends. The economy does not justify itself by serving itself. AT&T, IBM do not justify themselves by getting bigger. I am trying to answer Goldman's question about the meaning of the general welfare. What I understand Ferry to be saying is that the economy is here to serve society, and is not an end in itself. When we got an economic recession, the President said—as was said in 1932—it is your duty to go out and buy a car. It makes no difference whether you need one or not. You ought to buy a car because the economic order is an end in itself and we have to keep it going. I take it that Ferry is saying this is not so and should not be so.

GOLDMAN: We can take it to mean that, but he in no place has told us what the other ends are. He has made a first step in these statements, but not the significant step.

HUTCHINS: He tells you that you have to produce goods and services under conditions assuring just and rational production and just and equitable distribution.

FERRY: I did not take it as my assignment to do the work of this group. The Consultants are supposed to decide over the long term the elements of a good society. This paper is the Project on the Corporation speaking. The Project was asked to deal with those aspects of the good society concerned with getting and spending.

GOLDMAN: When you tell me that the ends are just and equitable distribution, you have not told me anything that means anything. I don't know what "just" means. I don't know what "equitable" means. Therefore, the step that we have made is, as I see it, to say that the economy does not exist for itself. It exists for some larger purposes, period.

HUTCHINS: That is right.

GOLDMAN: I don't think that takes us as far as our task requires us to go.

BUCHANAN: Might I try a narrowing definition of general welfare? It seems to me that general welfare in this context means what is necessary in the public sector of the economy. General welfare is a constitutional principle here, and it does not go to the point of seeing that General Motors is prosperous. That is not the same at all.

NIEBUHR: Brown thinks that this is an implied collectivism or an implicit collectivism. The Argument says that whatever mechanisms or controls are necessary to hold the economy to its proper purposes are just and proper. Goldman rightly says this does not define what is just and proper, but let us pass that for the moment. Everything that Brown objects to could be corrected by suggesting that, as Rabi says, the government necessarily must not have absolute power over these things. The Argument also includes formal planning by the national government to protect and promote the general welfare. What is lacking is the *modus vivendi* that we are always after; that is, you have to allow for some automatic processes. Wherever there are self-regulating features in the economy, you don't condemn them but appreciate them and don't interfere with them, because you don't want to have too much explicit control, which would lead to all kinds of new evils.

MURRAY: All that the first sentence in Proposition 7 asserts, stripped down, is that economic forces within society possess no absolute autonomy but are subject to some manner of higher regulation which can only be in terms of the exercise of the political power.

NIEBUHR: That is the first sentence. Then it goes on and says this includes formal planning by the national government.

MURRAY: Here we have descended from the level of principle as such to the level of fact. I take the real premise here to be a factual premise; that under present situations of disorder, confusion, chaos, and what not, there must be some sort of formal planning. Is that right?

FERRY: We are descending to the level of fact, but it strikes me that the footnote from the Guaranty Trust Company's bulletin shows how rapidly we move from the point of fact to crucial economic theory. The Guaranty editor says, "In a free society protected against violence and fraud, economic growth is an automatic process," and so forth. My statement about formal planning is an attack on automatic growth as the ruling condition of the American economy, on the idea that any way the economy works is fine as long as government keeps its hands off.

MURRAY: Of course, the real trap is the word "planning." That is what I meant by the political usurping what are properly economic functions. I am not myself at all sure that plans for economic growth or plans for economic decrease really fall within the political function. I am not convinced at all about a descent by government from its own level onto the level of the economy and operating as an economic power.

BUCHANAN: Suppose the planning were as formal as laws and duly passed by right authorities?

MURRAY: That would be something else again. Then one would have to take a look at the content and purpose of the law. Government would be on its proper level if planning were to be confined to legislative action of some sort or another.

FERRY: We have such a law in the Employment Act of 1946.

MURRAY: You have it in the whole tax structure. You have it in lots of forms of anti-monopoly legislation and so on. This is all right.

FERRY: I do not want to set up the Russian threat, so-called, as an important part of this argument. If the figures that we now have before us are correct, the Communist economies are growing at a rate of 7 to 10 per cent, and we are growing at a rate of 2 to 3 per cent. Is this something of which we ought, as a society and therefore politically, to take some cognizance and do something about?

MURRAY: Government should do something about it.

FERRY: By appropriate policies, legislation, or whatever?

MURRAY: I am not at all convinced of that off-hand.

HUTCHINS: Suppose you were to take a preliminary stage here? Suppose a governmental group were established by law for the purpose of analyzing and criticizing the economy and projecting a proper future. Suppose it were simply advisory. How do you feel about that?

MURRAY: I wouldn't feel unhappy about that. I start with the premise that the stability of the economy must inevitably be in some sense a concern of the government. How the concern manifests itself and the value of the mechanism would depend on whether it was duplicating a lot of other things that were going on. The government might say, leave it to the Rockefeller Brothers.

HUTCHINS: On the one hand, you would not object to laws constitutionally adopted that affected the economy like the anti-trust laws or the tax structure. On the other extreme, you would not object to something like the Board of Economic Advisors, which now exists and writes an annual report. What you are questioning then must be something in between the two. Suppose that the powers of the Federal Trade Commission were expanded; or suppose that the National Resources Planning Board were in existence and were given some authority so that it could actually allocate resources of one kind or another instead of having only the right to advise. It is this non-legislative yet quasi-legislative body having authority that you would question, is that correct?

MURRAY: What would they be empowered to do?

HUTCHINS: If they were more than an advisory body, they might have to begin with natural resources. They might be required to consider what could be done to get more schools and fewer lipsticks produced. This might carry over into allocation of labor. The thing that everybody always talks about is the control of wages and prices, both said to be indispensable to any kind of public planning. I would give them any powers that you think are necessary to carry out the provisions of this document, namely, general welfare, just and equitable distribution, just and rational production, and the conformity of corporations to standards of justice and freedom.

MURRAY: All those are difficult questions, especially for me, since I don't know much about this whole business. The words "just," "rational," "equitable," have a nice political moral ring, and therefore I would look upon government as a function or custodian of the justice of the economy. I would not consider it custodian, necessarily, of the growth of the economy. If manifest injustices occur, then it would seem appropriate for government to exercise its proper function.

You have to be a little careful always in these matters about how far you are going to push it. Should the government, whether on federal or state level, assign doctors to particular regions on their graduation from medical school? That would be a parallel in the professional sphere to some of the instances that have been brought up of labor allocation or materials allocation. I would not only be dubious but initially quite opposed to any such governmental action.

FERRY: What would you say if it could be shown, continuing your example, that great stretches of the United States were either totally without or had totally inadequate medical service while Park Avenue had four doctors to every twenty-five people?

MURRAY: This is not anything that government ought to meddle in.

HUTCHINS: It does meddle with it now.

HOFFMAN: It creates in the tax structure at least a system which encourages one kind of medical practice and discourages another. Legislation is responsible through things like the Social Security Act for one sort of encouragement of medical practice and discouragement of another sort.

MURRAY: If you say that is a fact, all right. I don't know one way or another.

68

HUTCHINS: Suppose you take a simpler one. Take the housing question. There is no doubt that government intervention in the housing field has had tremendous effects. Whether they are good or bad is another question. Housing activity on the part of the government has been engaged in without much regard for the rest of the economy, except as there are said to be mysterious coordinating bodies in Washington that we can only hope co-ordinate. Yet housing is supposed to have tremendous influence throughout the whole economy. So you have a very large govern-mental activity that is affecting the economy just as drastically as any general plan could, which is itself unplanned.

HOFFMAN: Isn't the example of the housing field useful to this problem of general welfare and justice because clearly the gov-ernmental policies in regard to federally supported housing have an effect on the availability of housing to people of various colors? The practice of the government over a long period of time has been not to disturb—in the Guaranty Trust Company's words— the existing automatic race and housing pattern. Yet any standard of justice and equity conforming to the Constitution would suggest that the government ought not to interfere with the economy on any basis other than to make equally available to people of all colors whatever the government services were.

MURRAY: Doesn't the matter of prudence come in there some-where along the line?

HOFFMAN: If you introduce the matter of prudence, you are then introducing things that you are not so sure you would like. You might say government should not go into Los Angeles with FHA mortgage loans which upset the behavior of Los Angeles banks and real estate agents in providing housing to Negroes. You might say that if a Negro wants to buy a house in Beverly Hills and gets an FHA loan on it, the government ought to see to it that the Negro does not get the FHA loan because the real estate agents and the banks won't like it. This would be prudent, I suppose, in one sense. The government would stay out of a lot of trouble.

GOLDMAN: I think this is relevant. The difficulty with the agency of criticism suggested in the *Notes* is that it pre-judges the role of the corporation. It pre-judges that there is some fixed role in our society for the corporation. It might be that the role of the corporation is not fixed at all, that the corporation simply should do at various times the different things which no other agency of our society can do, or can do as well or can do as quickly and so on. Therefore, this critical agency could not function. It has no criteria. It has no working papers, so to speak.

HUTCHINS: Ferry quotes the other Lincoln slogan, that the government should do for the people what they cannot do as well for themselves. This supports the earlier point that government is in the economic system up to its neck in various unrelated and related ways. There is no general theory under which the government participates in the economic order, because it is all done in response to pressure. What I am trying to find out is what the difference is between the way in which the government now participates in the economic order and the way in which the government might participate in the economic order if it said it was now going to try to participate rationally over the whole economic front. This would not mean it would participate uniformly. It might go very deep in housing at one time and not at all in another.

GOLDMAN: On the basis of what criteria?

HUTCHINS: You would start with the pragmatic question: What needs to be done?

GOLDMAN: Let us take our doctors. What criterion is going to permit an agency to say that the government ought to do this or that, rather than the AMA?

HUTCHINS: There are all kinds of ways in which the government can participate. At the present time in some states there are scholarships offered for medical students on condition that they return and practice a certain number of years in the state. Is that governmental intervention? I would say it was. Is it objectionable government intervention? I would say not, not even if I accepted, as I think I don't quite, Father Murray's attitude toward governmental control. It is not necessary to suppose that you are going to have a system of allocations of men, resources, and materials directed from a central governmental agency in order to accept the kind of thing that Ferry is here proposing.

FERRY: I perceive that the *Notes* have not sufficiently illuminated this situation. The amount of planning, government interference, intervention, assistance, whatever it may be called, is mammoth in this country. We accept it as a matter of course. It is only when attention is drawn to it, or one of the semaphores like the word "planning" is run up, that people become attentive and begin to think about it. Consider the recent order restricting oil imports into this country. This is planning on a large scale. We are all going to pay a little more for gasoline and fuel. It affects millions of people. I have heard no shouts about this. There have been a few letters in the newspapers. The comments have not been against this order as planning or as government intervention, but against those independent oil operators and their lobby in Washington.

There is a great deal of support all around us for Father Murray's statement about the primacy of the political order. I think it goes without saying that this is accepted as long as nobody has to speak about it. Even the man who wrote this *Guaranty Survey* editorial realizes that he is talking about a world that never was, even twenty-five years ago.

GOLDMAN: If I may try to get this on what seems to me a more general level, the *Notes* seem to me to ignore what has been the essential genius of our system. I am trying to describe it in a figure of speech — the occurrence of vacuums which in time are filled through a process of expediency by various types of instrumentalities. What is necessary are forms of pressure to get somebody to fill the vacuums, since we know the profit motive is not the whole story. It seems to me that has inherent in it a better way of doing things for the general welfare than any official agency could possibly have.

FERRY: What form of pressure are you talking about?

GOLDMAN: Let us take the question of the minimum wage laws. The government got in there a little bit. Welfare capitalism got in there a little bit. Insurance policies in a sense got in there a little bit. A whole battery of different kinds of things filled that particular vacuum.

FERRY: Speak a little bit about public parks, water pollution, air pollution, schools, highways, similar things. Most of us would agree that these words signify prominent vacuums in society right now. Mr. Galbraith has brought this out more clearly than has been done before. What pressures are being built up or will be built up, and by whom, to fill these vacuums?

GOLDMAN: The first pressure usually is that somebody says something about it in a way that makes other people talk about it. Pressure has been started by Mr. Galbraith's book.

FERRY: Up to this point these vacuums have existed. They can't really be vacuums by definition because, under your theory, something would have rushed in, would it not?

GOLDMAN: They don't rush in immediately. Perhaps vacuum is a bad figure of speech. "Deficiency" is a better word. What I am trying to avoid is the kind of agency which would practically dictate that the deficiencies would always be filled by the government.

RABI: I am reminded of this example by an ad I saw somewhere by the people who make the Rambler. They describe the public service they fulfill because the big companies were giving only these big cars, and this gave American Motors a way of satisfying a need. I am now talking in purely economic terms where apparently most of the economy went off base. That is something that started a swing the other way.

HUTCHINS: It costs a lot of money to learn this way.

FERRY: Suppose Mr. Romney had not come along and we continued to build big cars. It costs a lot of money. Highways have to be widened. All sorts of garages and parking lots become obsolete because of the size of these cars. You say this is a natural and unavoidable change in society under your scheme. Let us go back to the other point, because I must grant there is something to what you say. I don't like the use of the word "dictatorial" either. But certainly a part of the Argument would lead to a decision by society, acting through government, that these deficiencies ought to be filled whether or not there seems to be a lot of pressure to fill them.

Even if the people of this country appear to desire lipsticks more than public parks and schools and clean rivers, they still ought to have public parks and schools and clean rivers. This seems to me to be of the essence. I regard this as what is meant by the primacy of politics—taking the better, the longer view of the real needs of the community.

JACOBS: I would assume you are not in favor of planning just for the sake of planning, but planning when necessary and after calculating what risks are run to the individual and the society by the consequences of the planning. It is conceivable, even though you may solve some short-run need of some group with planning, in the long run the consequences may be disastrous for the whole of society. Would you agree with that?

FERRY: Yes. If I may refer to the earlier apprehension about the medical student and the allocation of his labor by the government by whatever device, I remind you that this is going on on a very large scale already in our high schools. We say to the kids in the ninth grade, you pick your vocational track. What do you want to be? A welder? All right, we will train you as a welder, and we do. In my view these early vocational choices are all condemnations to prison terms in particular trades. This method has nothing whatever to do with the equality of opportunity or with the equality of status. It has everything to do with the allocation of human resources at a very, very early age, and with the help of government. I am opposed to it. One finds, strangely enough, that these very schools are celebrated as the epitome of the democratic process at work.

I will say, however, that in Detroit and elsewhere the industrialists who are supposed to be served by these technical schools are having some grave second thoughts about it, so much so that last year a group of Ford, Chrysler, GM, and other industrialists reported to the Detroit Board of Education their conclusion that it would be on the whole better if technical and vocational training courses for both boys and girls were cut way back. They said, in effect, try to send us some educated people and we will do the training through apprenticeship courses. This is a tremendous reversal, because Detroit was the place that had the vocational education system tied up to the factory system and had made the biggest single jump into vocational training.

BUCHANAN: I wonder if I could return to the question of the distinction between economics and politics. I was asking whether there would be objections to planning if it were formulated as law. It seems to me this is the crucial point. Planning, as I understand it, has arisen from the habits of the managers, let us say the corporate managers, but I think it goes much farther than that. It is a term that comes from management more than from anywhere else. It came from Russia, too, in the early part of the Revolution. Even there it was taken from some European managerial notions. As it was posed in the New Deal, it was an administrative device. As we know, administrative law has not yet acquired real status in our legal system. We do not know quite what it is. We don't know whether there are safeguards of due process, for example.

The problem on planning may be one of reformulating due process and judicial aspects. You are admitting that the government has obligations about the economy of some kind or another that it has to discharge in some way or another. You are saying that this has to be done through law and not through running things or controlling them in a heavy sense at all but by creating some kind of orderly procedure.

MURRAY: One step farther back—correcting malfunctions of one sort or another.

BUCHANAN: That would be the occasion for it. Wouldn't you think this might have to become permanent? The disturbances and miscarriages of private enterprise at present are so frequent and general and systematic that it looks as if we ought to have more legal understanding. The law might consist in setting up institutions which would have a chartered or constitutionalized framework within which they would operate. The government would not be initiating and fixing up things at all. It would merely be saying: If you are going to discharge this function in society, you have to do it in this way.

MURRAY: As of the moment the government barges in here, there, and somewhere else all over the lot, at the instance of demonstrated need, let us say for the sake of argument. This has been accepted. I have no particular trouble accepting it in principle, give or take a particular instance where you might disagree about the need. Then, Hutchins went on to say, if it is all right for government to operate in this *ad hoc* fashion, what is wrong with its taking one step higher and exercising some sort of general superintendence over the whole business?

BUCHANAN: Superintendence is a strong word.

HUTCHINS: That is too strong for me, too.

BUCHANAN: I want strictly a legal process involved.

MURRAY: You defend these interventions on the ground that there is malfunction, that there is some manner of injustice in equity that has to be corrected. Indeed, it often happens that in correcting this malfunction here and getting it functioning something goes wrong somewhere else and you tinker. This is a kind of sloppy way to do things. Indeed, it does not look awfully rational, but maybe this is the thing that you do. This is where the word "planning" is bad. It is not enough to say that it is all right for government to intervene in the mode of law. What I am against is some dream or image of the world or the country as it ought to be which we will now fulfill by appropriate steps.

BUCHANAN: Suppose it is a vision but not a dream? Suppose your technological system is what is creating all these problems? The innovations bring on crises. I don't mean necessarily the big depressions but a crisis of operation and understanding between the people involved. Shouldn't the government take cognizance and find some regular way of dealing with innovations in technology?

MURRAY: I do think now you are getting very close to the heart of the problem. Technology is at the root of a great deal of disorder, the disorder being systematic in itself and being created systematically.

BUCHANAN: That is right.

MURRAY: If this is the situation, and perhaps it is, then I certainly would think it is time to sit back and say maybe something big has got to be done about this. This new force has to be understood and provided with a proper harness of a legal kind.

HUTCHINS: I would like to suggest the opposite of this. Take the Federal Reserve Board at the present time. By opening and closing valves on credit, it can do almost anything. Moreover, it does it in complete secrecy as far as I can see. Rumors appear in the press about what the Federal Reserve is going to do. Usually they don't do it. They do something else. Since they don't want to affect the markets adversely, they act with complete secrecy and expedition. The Federal Reserve is an attempt on the part of people whom we used to call Wall Street in my youth to impose their vision of the economy on the country. It is done by a very large staff of expert planners. It goes right to the heart of the economic system, doesn't it?

MURRAY: Have they a vision, these people? I should think so.

HUTCHINS: I think they have one.

GOLDMAN: I think your illustration indicates what might be wrong with this idea of a government planning agency. As I understand the Federal Reserve story, pressure came for it with exactly Ferry's purpose in mind. Not entirely or even primarily from Wall Street.

HUTCHINS: It was Carter Glass.

GOLDMAN: Yes. It was from people who wanted to see what could be done. What it turned into is an agency that can't do anything except through governmental action.

HUTCHINS: The situation is a lot better than it was before the Federal Reserve.

GOLDMAN: This may be.

HUTCHINS: My point is that here you have a powerful agency very seldom heard of. I imagine there is not anyone here who can name more than one member of the Federal Reserve Board, other than the Chairman. These people control the economic system of this country. This is not altered by the fact that many of the things they do have the opposite effect from that which they intended.

BUCHANAN: This is an illustration of a process that has not become legal.

HUTCHINS: Precisely. I think this is not a legal process in the sense that it is really arbitrary.

BUCHANAN: This is the case with a good many bureaus. You can multiply that.

HUTCHINS: The FCC is a classical example.

MURRAY: Suppose I say it calls for this particular kind of expert gadgetry. There is no other way of moderating or controlling or imparting some stability to the economy except in terms of a control of credit exercised by some such board of experts, supposedly disinterested, but not necessarily infallible people. Either this or chaos.

HUTCHINS: Take the figure that Stuart Chase has used, I think about twenty years ago. The economy is sixty billion wild horses.

Without taking this very literally it does suggest—and this bears on the technology point—120 billion wild horses and God knows how many more tomorrow. How is this to be handled in the public interest?

HOFFMAN: Ought we not to interfere with anything, or ought we not to bring the power of government into economic decision-making unless it is clear something is functioning badly? Ought we first to wait until something goes wrong, or it is clear that something is about to go wrong? Isn't this just the program of the Guaranty Trust Company, that the processes of the economy must be automatic? But it is the most automatic thing in the world for us to go to the government and try to have government intervene in our behalf. The whole operation of the government in the economy at the moment, it seems to me, is the result of groups of one sort or another bringing about governmental intervention in their own interests.

It is possible to say that the economy is almost entirely managed by government and almost entirely managed by people who do not know what the other managers are doing. A rational view of the self-interest of the economy, for instance, would probably conclude that if we are in any danger of oil shortage, we certainly would not want to restrict oil imports. The argument for the restriction of oil imports is that we are in danger of an oil shortage. Because we restrict the imports, therefore we are going to stimulate people to find more oil in the ground some place in the interior of the United States. This seems to me to be a peculiar and irrational argument, and it has nothing to do with the Texas Oil Commission, the California Commission, and the rest of the government agencies that are operating on the oil business.

JACOBS: Buchanan, you said you wanted to regularize this procedure by law. You mean to remove it from politics?

BUCHANAN: No, put it in politics in the upper brackets.

HUTCHINS: Take the FCC, for example; what is the real trouble? I would say the real trouble is the law. It is a terrible law. Not only is it a terrible law, but the courts have not helped. If you could straighten the FCC out legally, you might be under way. The whole thing rests on three words, "public interest, convenience, and necessity." Neither the courts nor the Commission nor Congress have ever made anything out of these words. So there is nothing, for all practical purposes, but a series of rulings that can't be defended.

MURRAY: This is one of the classic arguments for the limitation of governmental and legal intervention. The law is a very crude instrument. Even granted the highest legal craftsmanship, the drawing of statutes is notoriously imprecise. This being so, let us not use it unless there is a clear-cut kind of business that we can meet in a clear-cut way.

HUTCHINS: In this case everybody had to agree that there had to be a law. You had a limited number of frequencies; they had to be allocated by somebody; they could be allocated only by the government, and hence it had to be done by law. But the criteria established were so bad, the law was so poor and has been so poorly interpreted, that what you really have is a non-legal or at most semi-legal government for this institution that is becoming larger and larger and in some ways more and more significant in the national life.

MURRAY: What you are saying in effect is that the people who made the law were rather stupid, and perhaps they were. At any rate, they could not foresee the future.

HUTCHINS: There is a more likely explanation. It is not that the law was drafted stupidly. It is because we in this country, even in so clear a case as electronic communications, hate the idea of the government's having any kind of role in something in which money is involved. This law has been distorted, twisted, defeated at every turn. As we all know, the Federal Communications Commission is dominated by the financial interests that control the networks.

BUCHANAN: Yet Ferry is taking away from the corporation its capacity for discovering and formulating its purpose. But he is giving it to the government, which is obviously incapable of dealing with the big economic, military, and other problems that arise. This re-allocation of functions is a depressing sight. I mean depressing in the same way that Sweden is depressing. When you turn this all over to the government as is done in Sweden, you get a very dull, not necessarily stupid, kind of society.

What I am thinking of, as some of you are guessing, is that you don't hand such a function over to the government—the national government. You hand over this function to a new kind of corporation which is chartered to determine its own function and legalize its own operation—a self-governing body. This might be some federal scheme. You would not have one national economic corporation. You would have 200 or 500 corporations, or whatever they are, and some kind of congress of corporations that would deal with political-economic matters through legal means.

GOLDMAN: What makes you believe—if the corporations do not serve the general welfare now — that if you organize them more tightly and give them more power they will serve the general welfare better?

BUCHANAN: This is an old article of faith I find in the Constitution. You do not in this country order things from Washington and have them happen in Richmond, Virginia. On the whole, the federal government takes the position that if you organize the local community and protect it in its political operations, it will serve the common good.

GOLDMAN: You and I always have had a different reading of the Constitution. I assume the Constitution is based on the principle that the way to keep a good society is to keep its various parts all worrying each other. You have another assumption.

BUCHANAN: You say pluralism was written into the Constitution, and I deny it with all the strength I have. I say federation was.

BUCHANAN: The big division at present is between public and private corporations. The public ones are supposedly under a rule of law. The private ones are not strictly under rule of law; they are merely chartered without any definition of purpose or any rules of procedure. A charter is in effect just a license to operate. The public utility corporation has the peculiar status of both. It is private in ownership and you might say public in operation. It is the only corporation in which serving the public is a stated purpose.

The private corporations are of two kinds, the profit corporations and the non-profit. We were discussing yesterday what right a private corporation has to make donations to charitable corporations, universities, and so forth. This comes from a deep symbiotic relation these two kinds of corporations have. There is a quid pro quo between them. Take just the fact that a great deal of our technological advance comes from research done in universities and colleges. The business corporation has a kind of debt it owes to the universities for this reason. It somehow discharges public responsibility if it gives money to a charitable corporation, and not merely to universities but to other kinds, too. This makes me think that the profit corporation is a kind of fragment of something larger that might be organic and institutionally sound.

We had a paper here not long ago entitled "The Sickness of the Corporation." The thesis was that a profit corporation throws up its problems to us at present because it is a sick institution. It is groping around for something to do. This responsibility is a symptom of a kind of illness or decay inside the corporation. The author is saying that corporations in the past have operated healthily as long as they felt their dependence on the government and on the society. Whenever they became independent they went out of existence. He suggests it may be a suicidal thing for a corporation to take on sovereignty in the way that our corporations are doing at present.

I am not sure I agree with that thesis. My notion is almost the opposite; that is, the corporation is sick because it does not know its own purpose, and that the way for it to discover its purpose is to think about itself in terms of the rule of law.

This would mean that the corporation think of itself literally as a government, as Berle has put it often enough, and try to constitutionalize itself in some way. This doesn't necessarily mean that we should impose a democratic dogma on it. It means that the corporation, if it isn't going to be democratic, should say it is not going to be and find a mode of operation that will discharge its responsibilities and be efficient in its own operation. Ferry, however, seems to be saying corporations are never going to discover this purpose. It has to be told what its purpose is by the government, and held to it by the government. This is the alternative to what I am speaking of.

HUTCHINS: You say that the alternatives are either that the corporation should think about itself in terms of the rule of law and, therefore, constitutionalize itself, or that somebody else—inevitably the government—has to think about it and tell it what its purposes are and arrange for such constitutional amendments as are necessary.

BUCHANAN: There are two possibilities. One is to give the corporation a constitution and a rule of law within its own body; second, to change the federal Constitution or state constitutions in such a way that they regulate and take their full responsibility with relation to corporations.

82

NIEBUHR: What would this rule of law say to the corporation other than what the law says now?

BUCHANAN: The corporation is chartered for profit only. This is a faulty formulation. It doesn't seem to me that "for profit" is a purpose. It is saying something about how it operates, but it is not saying what it is operating for.

MURRAY: You grant "for profit" does rank as a private purpose.

BUCHANAN: It doesn't seem to me it could be even that.

MURRAY: If the purpose of the corporation is profit alone, I think it would rank as a private purpose. In that case it is a little difficult to see how, without stretching things a lot, you are going to bring it under governmental control, except insofar as injustice or damage or something else might arise from the pursuit of a private purpose. If you say to the government, "All I want to do is make money; you just leave me alone," you might have something to say about laws of competition and various other practices. If this thing has only a private purpose, under what formula do you bring it under the sovereignty of the state?

FERRY: The state would enter at many gates. Operating for profit does not mean operating completely without the oversight or the control of the state. The state would make sure, as it does at present, that labor is not mistreated, underpaid, injured. The state would step in as it may step into the steel situation if the prices charged have an unwarranted bad effect on the general welfare.

MURRAY: Under some sort of Lockean formula that I may pursue my own private purposes and exercise my private rights as long as no damage is done to the right of others.

BUCHANAN: The corporation now operates under common law rules about the ownership of property and the enforcement of contracts. Government will protect property, it will enforce contracts. The corporation can operate in this way. There is no particular reason for having a charter under those circumstances. "Charter" is a kind of vestigial symbol of a public purpose. The presumption is still strong that a corporation exists because its purpose is something that the government wants to encourage. It doesn't want to operate it; it doesn't want to regulate it very much; but it gives a charter for whatever the corporation will do for the public good.

NIEBUHR: Why couldn't you say that the corporation is a quasi-sovereignty and the public charters it on the old principle that you have to harness it for the sake of the public good? Why should one turn back to the old pure economic self-regard—profit—and say this makes it neater? It does make it neater, but life is not neat. So what you are dealing with is a quasi-sovereignty, as with a labor union.

Then you try to figure out how this quasi-sovereignty, seeking its own ends, can serve the public interest. You don't do that by going back to the original economic motive. There is more than economic motive there. All you have to do is to guarantee that the public ends will be served, and that the private ends will be harnessed for the public interests. That is done in terms of regulating quasi-sovereignties, rather than regulating motives.

MURRAY: I presume you are not supporting the French theory that no intermediate institutions are allowed to exist between state sovereignty and the individual, that all power is concentrated in the sovereign. There can be no quasi-sovereigns existent below him except at his good pleasure.

BUCHANAN: But at his good pleasure there can be. It seems to me that is the origin of the corporation, if I understand the history. That is exactly what happened. That was the understanding of the sovereign when he made the first charters for the big corporations.

NIEBUHR: You must allow quasi-sovereignties, whether they are corporations, church, educational institutions. The more quasi-sovereignties you have, the better protection you have against totalitarianism. The paradox is that extreme individualism makes for

84

an extreme totalitarianism, because the state does not allow any sovereignty except its own.

MURRAY: It is one thing for me to walk up to the door of government and say, please, Mr. Government, I would like to start a corporation. Do you mind? My hands are tied. It is another thing for me to say to government, I have started a corporation, and obviously it exists in the society and there is danger of conflict, and obviously we are going to deal in contracts, and obviously several other things. Therefore, I acknowledge that you, the guardian of the order of law, can use legitimately the long arm of the law to touch me in many respects. But for my existence or the justification for my existence I can appeal to another source. What I am going to do is a contribution to the public good, not the public good in so far as it is directly committed to government, but the public good as involved in the general concept of prosperity. I am going to help make this society prosperous by producing wealth. On the other hand, I can't be a cancer in the body politic. You are allowed to do a little surgery now and again if I exceed my bounds, general rules of justice and human rights must be enforced by government, and so on. These are two different things.

BUCHANAN: I think corporations are touched with this contradiction at this time and this is their uncertainty.

NIEBUHR: I think that the virtue would lie in the contradictions.

MURRAY: I don't like this notion of contradiction being a good thing. I think things inherently contradictory are doomed in the end.

NIEBUHR: Leaving out economic life, take the political party. Any political party says it exists in order to establish the common good. That is its purpose. Any good politician wants to have the victory of his party, but he also wants the good of the commonwealth.

MURRAY: These two things are not contradictory. What he wants to do may very well be for the public good.

BUCHANAN: There is a much sharper contradiction between profit only and public service in the corporation. By strict legal terminology I take it the only purpose that the corporation can have is to make profit. This is slipping pretty badly now.

RABI: We treat the corporation to some extent as having the rights or responsibilities of an individual. Particularly there is an overtone of moral responsibility. I don't understand in theory how a corporation which does not have a soul or conscience can be said to have certain responsibilities, and how you attach responsibilities to such a zombie.

HUTCHINS: Lord Thurlow said that the corporation had no backside to be kicked.

NIEBUHR: That is no different from the nation. Does the nation have a conscience or doesn't it have a conscience?

RABI: It does not help me to transfer the problem to the nation. I have always been worried by the point that the nation as such has some outside responsibility, that because we are rich, we have a moral responsibility to other nations. I don't know how to put it in moral terms. I can see it in terms of policy. But this is a different matter.

BERLE: I wonder if we are not over-complicating. The history of chartering is an amusing one. In the early days of the Roman Empire, the Emperor demanded a license of every body corporate primarily on the theory that he wanted to know what was going on. In the early English time, they were chartered primarily as a way of getting something done that the state wanted done. Then they got out of hand and prohibitive legislation was enacted, as in 1720 after the South Sea Bubble burst. Corporations were practically blanked out for a little over a hundred years in English life. The theory was that they were too dangerous. Then they began to come in favor again. The charter is only a device for getting them recognized and created. It is a device for giving them certain privileges. It is a device for getting certain things done.

It is also a device for prohibiting certain things.

In our phase of it, these corporations were chartered to make money, but to make money by doing particular things. The profit motive was not the be-all and end-all. Certain things had to be done in order to get that. That was the social utility theory. We are just coming into the next phase. As I see it, corporations were to do several things: supply a market, develop the art, gather savings—that last is new. With 60 per cent of the industrial capital of the country gathered through corporations, you begin to see that they have acquired a function in the last thirty years that was unknown earlier. This is a function they acquired without knowing it. The old common law rule against trusts was thought of as a device for controlling prime capital gatherers. Now there is a new situation, one part of which is obviously a terrific desire to make jobs and maintain stability.

It appears that increasingly we are coming to a point in which the corporation is to submit itself to and become an active and assisting member of some planning mechanism of some kind. We are coming into the national planning mechanism now. At the same time come some negative aspects. The corporation must not steal from its stockholders, it is not to exploit its customers, it is not to exploit its labor. It is supposed not to discriminate in buying or selling. It must not monopolize. It must not grow too big, although the anti-trust cases are shifting. It must not contribute too much to political campaigns, and the length and breadth of that becomes pretty indefinite, too.

The traditional democratic process that we know about in politics does not work very well within a corporation for practical purposes, so there are oligarchies. These are kept in control by a public consensus which at any given moment may discipline the corporation with varying degrees of severity. That is the existing system as far as we can see it, and it is this consensus which gives any "democratic" concept to corporations some validity. It has compelled the development of machinery by which it can be applied— the regulatory commissions, for example. The consensus is beginning now to demand some kind of planning.

MURRAY: Would this generalization be permitted, that the interventions of law are in the form of negative commands? Thou shalt not do thus and so. The positive purposes and dynamisms of the corporation are generated, as it were, from within. They receive some authorization, because they are active in the public domain.

It has to do with the difference between the statements, I qualify you for existence, or, I watch over you and stop you from doing various kinds of things. You did have quite a number of thou shalt nots; is it true to say that the government intervenes only in this negative way?

BERLE: None of these things appears in charters. I don't know a charter that says anywhere in it thou shalt not overcharge, or thou shalt not exploit labor. It came from the outside. The corporation is organized because somebody hopes to make some money out of it, or to become a great and powerful figure. This has been the dynamic urge unquestionably. It also is true that the organizer expected to accomplish this by doing something considered useful at the time.

HUTCHINS: Doesn't the *quo warranto* proceeding assume that a corporation is authorized for a purpose, so that if it does not pursue that purpose it may be deprived of its charter?

BERLE: It is very rarely used. The last one I remember is when the Philadelphia Electric Company started to sell electric toasters and other things, and the dealers brought a proceeding asking by what right does a corporation chartered to sell electricity sell appliances.

HUTCHINS: It can only be brought by the state.

BERLE: Yes. It is an action by the Attorney General of the state at the initiation of somebody. As a practical matter, what happens today is that the state passes a general statute saying thou shalt not, whatever it is, employ women in factories more than so many hours, or what not. I suppose if the public consensus decided that such things were dangerous, you would have a rash of *quo war-ranto* suits again.

FERRY: Hasn't the phrase in the preamble of the Constitution "to promote the general welfare" been taken to mean that almost anybody, by means of a federal or state charter, could go into business as a corporation, subject to certain general prohibitions? Some of these are in the common law, some are explicit in state law. Aside from that, we think that the general welfare will be best promoted if we let you alone to find your own way, to fail or succeed on entirely commercial tests. Promoting the welfare means no more than that. It suggests no positive injunction such as that we require that you always make very good products, that you always sell at reasonable prices. No such requirements have ever been set out. Isn't that really the attitude this country has taken toward this phrase?

MURRAY: My basic concern was to find out the relation between Buchanan's concept of chartering corporations and what has been a sort of general theory with regard to voluntary organizations. Since they are organized within a larger political, social, economic system, they do and must come under the cognizance of law. What is the relationship? What is at stake really is the concept of the state.

BERLE: Suppose three of us here decided we would incorporate and we got up a charter and sent it to the Secretary of State, and he says, "We don't understand you fellows. I won't charter you." We would file a writ of mandamus to require the Secretary of State to stamp the charter and issue it, and it would be issued. There is no longer under our present system a matter of giving discretion to the state.

BUCHANAN: A minute ago you said that the corporation is coming into a field where planning has to be done either by the corporation in terms of the public good or else by the government assigning it.

BERLE: My present view is that planning is not a settlement of anything, but a forum within which conflicts can be settled. When people say planning is the answer to anything, they obviously have not thought it through. It only sets up machinery for settling conflicts which otherwise can be determined only by the open market or by the rule of power or something of that kind, with results you wish to avoid.

BUCHANAN: Could you say you are setting up a legal institution?

BERLE: That is exactly what it is.

MURRAY: This notion of planning obviously has something to do with the notion of order. You can look at it in two ways. A planner can have an antecedent vision of an order that he wants, or he can take cognizance of disorder and do a job of ordering. In the first case he is calling into substantive existence, perhaps for the first time, things that he has decided ought to be there. In the second case he just takes a look at what is there but sees it as a little chaotic, so he does a work of ordering. He is not constructing an order, he is simply ordering a conglomerate kind of thing that is there already.

BERLE: Your planning commission in that case is a body that maintains public order by lopping off the head of the fellow that seems to be making trouble at the time. Or you can have some criteria. That is why, the minute you say planning, you have to draw a careful set of criteria of what the planning is all about.

MURRAY: We have to have a theory with regard to your right to do this planning.

BUCHANAN: This is where the charter would be the instrument to do this.

BERLE: More likely a planning commission, a new growth in the constitutional law.

NIEBUHR: I interpret Berle's analysis like this: What we have to do is to harness not only individual self-interest but collective self-interest—corporations and labor unions. We have to interpret self-interest not only in economic terms but in all the terms you have elaborated and we elaborated previously. This is the heart of a liberal society, that it does not suppress immediate purposes, parochial interest, et cetera, et cetera, but harnesses them. It suppresses them when they are dangerous, but on the whole harnesses them. We always ask what is the ultimate purpose. That is the heart of liberalism. Against that you have totalitarianism. There is a contradiction between the ambition of a statesman and his desire or his usefulness in serving the common good. We don't rule out an "ambitious" statesman. That would rule out everybody. But if we say he is too ambitious, he is ruled out.

BUCHANAN: What is the contradiction in that?

NIEBUHR: If you were absolutely moral about it, you would say that nobody who serves his own interest rather than the common good, in motive, is doing the right thing for the state.

BUCHANAN: But they are connected.

NIEBUHR: That is the very heart of the liberal doctrine, that it is possible to harness self-interest for the common good. There was the medieval theory that it was simple to tell who the tyrant was. The tyrant was one who served his own interests rather than the state's interests. That made him a tyrant. That makes everybody a tyrant according to our conception. The very heart of an empirical, liberal society depends on confidence in a wisdom that transcends the wisdom of any of the actors or agents in the society. If you try to impose a wisdom upon this you always have a false wisdom. Take, for instance, the long struggle between monarchism and anti-monarchism. Out of this came the constitutional monarchy. That is not what either party intended, but it happens to be wiser than either side contended for. That is the wisdom of providence that transcends the wisdom of any of the actors.

HUTCHINS: What is the difference between providence and "bumps and grinds"?

NIEBUHR: There is not too much difference.

HUTCHINS: If "bumps and grinds" is so close to providence, why do we need to plan?

NIEBUHR: Insofar as man has the transcendence over circumstances and reason over circumstances to plan, he must plan. As far as he has not got as transcendent a reason as he thinks he has, he can't plan.

KERR: I want to agree with what Niebuhr was saying about the "bumps and grinds" theory. The emphasis should be on having a private sector in which anybody can make virtually any decision he wants to. Then there is a public sector also. You leave the line between them pretty hazy. Things can be moved back and forth depending on what works best. If you move something into the public sector, you try to structure the situation so that the most pressures can be brought to bear. In the trade unions at the present time the effort is to allow the members to bring more pressure than before.

When you talk about planning, you are really talking about structuring a society not so that there can be the maximum number of individual decisions, but rather to keep away from individual decisions. You have to tie it to some ideology to have real planning. The really planned society is one that is structured to minimize the individual decisions. The great struggle in the world at the present time is about which is the better way to structure society. It is not planning in the old "city plan" sense where you structure the city planning commission in such a way that it has to be responsive to the desires of many, many people.

NIEBUHR: Paul Appleby, the Assistant Secretary of Agriculture during the war, had a marvelous example of planning and limits of planning. He said they had a session in Washington where they came to an agreement that the way to prevent inflation in war was to increase certain agricultural production, particularly milk. So they planned, and they got an order from the War Production Board that they could have additional tractors for additional agricultural production. But then, unfortunately, the farmers would have none of the tractors. So they lost a lot of steel making tractors that nobody wanted. They simply did not recognize some of the contingent factors.

FERRY: Would you say this is the sort of experience one must expect out of planning on any scale larger than a city or state?

NIEBUHR: No. Take the planning that the Russians do, and the planning they did in Hungary and in Poland. They had an ideological scheme for their planning, namely, that collectivized agriculture would be more efficient than non-collectivized agriculture. They forced this scheme on Poland and on Hungary. The cost in human life and the cost in efficiency was tremendous. Poland has only now caught up in its dairy production. This is an ideological plan that was pressed upon all the contingent factors of history, including the preference of the peasant for the soil and for his own cattle, et cetera.

RABI: Let us talk about another kind of planning. When you plan a building, you really plan it. But every engineer knows he has to put in a factor of safety, simply because he does not know. Some time later you may discover that he put in too great a factor of safety and it cost 20 per cent too much. Or that he put in too little and the thing collapsed. As soon as you show that he put in too big a factor, and so it was a waste, or put in too small a factor and so it is criminal, then you have given up all idea of planning under circumstances which are contingent. I don't think you are right in saying that there was a waste of tractors. This will have to be always a part of planning. It won't work completely. Once you adjust yourself to the fact that this is a necessity of planning, then you can talk about planning in ordinary human terms.

NIEBUHR: You are quite right. Appleby said we must not plan too far down the line.

FERRY: I find most acceptable Berle's suggestion as to the meaning of planning, as a forum in which conflicts of importance to the nation can be worked out systematically. I do not think it is quite appropriate to talk about planning as automatically equaling the experience in Hungary and Russia. These really are the scare words.

HUTCHINS: Kerr was drawing a distinction between ideological and non-ideological planning. Couldn't we agree at once that no one expects to have ideological planning for the United States? The question is, what is the forum of non-ideological planning?

BERLE: Any planning will propose ideology whether you like it or not. The question is how far it goes. I accept Kerr's idea that the ideology is highly flexible.

GOLDMAN: Berle, you say the corporation may be entering a new phase because of this conception that unemployment is to be taken care of by planning. Is the talk of government-controlled planning, or that the corporations should themselves simply make some plan which they would control?

BERLE: There is no resolution of that. Any corporation will resist to the utmost the idea of "government planning." But if they can get together without being bumped by the anti-trust law, they will plan themselves; or they will try to work out a system of quotas for imports, or any other kind of thing that they think will produce the results they want. I think one piece of ideology is being pounded down; that is, that the system should offer employment to practically anybody that wants it practically all the time. That is a point on which, at the moment, the public consensus wants action. This is the immediate pressure for planning, although there are other pressures, too. There is no agreement as to how it ought to be done as yet.

GOLDMAN: Is this political talk or is it corporation talk?

BERLE: It is political talk primarily. I think there is a degree of resignation to it in the corporations. Corporation people seem to accept the general notion that this is coming down the road.

FERRY: You see some evidence of changing corporate attitudes.

94

Consider Mr. Romney's statement about the automobile industry. He says the government is going to have a choice of busting up General Motors and other major companies into competitive units, or becoming a protective agency for the likes of American Motors. Thereby the government would see that we get the products we need at prices that we can afford. If it takes a giant plan including allocation of resources to do so, that is all right, too. This seems to be Mr. Romney's cry from inside the corporation.

HUTCHINS: As I understand it, there is some agreement here that a certain kind of something called planning is necessary and inevitable. Ferry has suggested a sort of parallel procedure, that of institutionalized criticism. Have you any views that you care to express?

BERLE: The "planning" that we have been talking about is a mechanism by which some sort of general picture of the world and items of doctrine can be made effective. The institutionalized criticism that Ferry talks about really is a method for helping to develop a public consensus. It is a mechanism for the protection of individuals and with positive requirements for stating in a general way a democratic public consensus and helping thereby to raise sights all around. At this point systematic criticism becomes of enormous importance.

FERRY: The proposal for this independent agency arises out of a conviction that we are moving very much faster than almost anyone realizes. We cannot understand this accelerating rate of change under the present conditions of criticism. I don't think, for example, that it is possible for any of us to appraise the extent to which technology is affecting us.

GOLDMAN: Your proposal goes further than that. This agency would operate on a theory of the corporation. It would then look at the corporations and judge to what extent they are operating as proper instruments under the theory.

FERRY: That would be one of the tasks. Criticism could not

emerge from a vacuum. It would have to come from a theory of the economic organization of the society and what the proper place of the corporation — especially the large corporation — should be.

GOLDMAN: I should think there would hardly be any objection to a group of wise and knowledgeable men saying, this is the way things are going, adding to public information, and thereby presumably creating a healthier public opinion. But if they are going to operate on a theory of society, I would argue that the very setting up of the group prejudges what the theory is going to be.

HUTCHINS: Do you agree with the proposition that there is no economic theory at the present time adequate to describe and explain the economic order?

GOLDMAN: Yes.

HUTCHINS: I understand Mr. Ferry's paper to suggest that the independent critical agency that might be established would have to direct its attention in the first instance to the fact that there is no theory, and would therefore have to try to develop one.

BERLE: Yes. My own picture would be that you have the critical agency, which is some more or less recognized method by which ideas are developed. It looks at the situation and at what is being done, and makes its findings. This really is a feeder for the public consensus. It increases the public consensus. It would be an accessory to a planning agency, if we formulated one, to the extent that it is needed. Systematic criticism would have a double function. On the one hand, it might crystallize consensus into public opinion on a particular problem or need; on the other, it might induce your planning agency or corporation—without recourse to intervention—to go ahead and get to work on it.

FERRY: I will accept all of that.

HUTCHINS: Let me see if I understand. You look forward, then, to two new institutions in society, one perhaps wholly private. This might be devoted to criticism and the development of theory and feeding the public consensus. The other would be wholly public, and would have the duty and the power to engage in the kind of planning we would try to discover from an examination of the record of this discussion. This would be a power to rationalize insofar as possible the operations of the economic system in the public interest.

BERLE: Yes.

HUTCHINS: Does everyone agree?

GOLDMAN: We have left the planning notion in such a stage that it could be anything.

HUTCHINS: I don't think quite, have we? There is one thing that is clear, and that is it is a public agency and has power. The precise nature of the power and the means of exercising it are certainly not fully clear. But these two things would seem to be indispensable. It is not a purely advisory body.

BERLE: Could I draw a picture as it seems to me? We now have about thirty different planning agencies in Washington, though not called by that name. They run all the way from the Civil Aeronautics Board, to executive action under oil import quotas, to the Federal Reserve Board. If you put all these together and tried to see that they act rationally, act together, and act with somewhat the same premises, you would begin to find that you had most of what you needed in national planning. If you added to that the purely advisory powers of the President's Board of Economic Advisors, you would discover, that so far as the mechanics are concerned, you had pretty much all that is required for the time being. What you need in addition might be some light on export and foreign aid and the whole overseas economic operation.

Then there is the critical body. At one time I hoped that the American Assembly would function in that capacity. A critical agency would help the various corporations to move to meet situations without having to be hammered over the head. The critical body could have, that is, tremendous authority, if not power. It could give accolade and censure, if you choose, to (a) the planning authority you speak of, or (b) the corporate people below. This would give both a feel of accountability and a feel of responsibility which I would think would be of considerable usefulness. At any rate, these are the institutional developments that I am tending toward.

FERRY: A Presidential Commission recommended that all foreign economic programs be brought under a single agency. The reason was the lack of coherence and the need for more system and more planning. This is significant, because this commission was made up of businessmen now involved in overseas aid, oil industry representatives, and the like. Their report is a direct call for planning, involving something in the neighborhood of 12 to 15 billion dollars' worth of exports.

BUCHANAN: Are you suggesting a growth or codification of administrative law?

BERLE: I hope it would not be codification at this stage. Of course, the real issues are strange. There is one anti-trust case going on now respecting foreign trade, in which it doesn't matter a whoop financially to most of the people involved. They can make the same money either way. The real question is where the actual jobs and manufacturing process will take place. The anti-trust people are anxious that they take place in the United States, and the profit-making enterprise does not care much. So you are fighting out a problem of where the jobs are. That is a thing that does not inhere in deep common law. That inheres in some process of decision.

BUCHANAN: It seems to me you might be overloading the administrative agencies under your scheme unless they are reorganized.

HUTCHINS: You would reorganize them?

BERLE: I hope so.

KERR: Don't we need to work toward a broader definition of

national economic health than we have had? The Council of Economic Advisors, reflecting what Congress is wanting and the public is wanting, has defined economic health as relatively full employment, and a good rate of increasing productivity.

BERLE: The question is whether they add to inflation.

KERR: Yes. They want relatively full employment, good productivity, and a relatively stable price structure. Suppose the Council of Economic Advisors were given a broader assignment by Congress, which would reflect broader desires by the public. You would say that national health ought to be defined also to include some ideas about the structure of the economy and some ideas also about the over-all use of national income—the percentage for education, the percentage for parks, as compared with the percentage, say, to consumers' goods. Don't we need to work somehow, within the public, within Congress, and within the Council of Economic Advisors, for a broader definition of what is economic health in the United States?

NIEBUHR: The trouble with that is that the Economic Advisors, which is a non-representative body, would have the authority to say we are giving too much for consumer goods and haven't got enough for other things. Could you imagine them doing that?

KERR: Supposing Congress gave them that assignment. The Congress gave them a narrow assignment of full employment. Suppose now we say economic health should be defined more broadly.

GOLDMAN: Doesn't this go to the question of how you get something done in our kind of society and whether this board has authority to say something that does not depend on public opinion? Ferry got to the position where he said if the public wants lipsticks rather than public parks, they should be given public parks.

FERRY: That is a rather free translation.

GOLDMAN: If the public at the present time is spending money on lipsticks rather than public parks, there is some presumption that they want the lipsticks rather than public parks.

FERRY: Just a minute. Are there no exceptions? Can't they have both?

NIEBUHR: That raises a fundamental question. For instance, Teller, the physicist, says the public should realize that our defense is more important than financing of automobiles and annual models. Should some representative body, some appointive body, say that to the public? I can't quite see anybody saying that to the public except a scientist.

RABI: How will the public say that they prefer this rather than that? It is not presented to them as an issue. How does the public say they don't like the narrow collars that we are getting on all clothing?

NIEBUHR: That is handled by the law of supply and demand.

RABI: No, there is no supply otherwise. It is an administrative thing. It is all you can get. How does the public say I prefer this or that to lipstick?

GOLDMAN: I think the analogy that Mr. Niebuhr has brought up is not exact. The issue there is: Do we want a good national defense? On that—that defense is important—the public consensus is clear. The argument is simply about how much money you have to spend to get a good national defense and many people have the opinion that we don't need to expend as much as we do to get it.

RABI: It is not as different as you say. When do we have enough bombs, when do we have a good national defense? In each case there is a certain kind of expertise that goes into it. To each case there will be a difference of opinion. These are not different points, except the one case that is presented with a great deal of force and the other case that is presented differently.

NIEBUHR: I don't want to be an authoritarian, but take the finance on the automobiles. The public obviously does not fervently desire finance. But the financing is a part of the competition in the automobile industry, and making automobiles is a great necessity in keeping the economy going. This is one of the ways that we subordinate the culture to the economy. But who is going to say we have an absolutely wrong system here? Yet we must put public defense first even if it should mean eliminating the annual models or something like that. I don't see the Economic Advisors saying that, do you?

KERR: No, I don't see them saying that. That would be going an awfully long way from what we have now. To set up a mechanism to control the style of automobiles you will have to have an authoritarian system.

FERRY: You have a very few people making such decisions now. No one can argue that the present design of automobiles is the product of democratic process.

HUTCHINS: Who decides that we get all these Westerns on television?

KERR: Not the "democratic process" if you mean by "democratic process" the decision by individual consumers. It is the result of our pluralistic system. Maybe there have not been enough pressures on the automobile companies. But we do have a slow way of bringing pressure upon these private authorities. That is the essence of our current system. I don't see how with the automobile industry you could have truly individual choice. You can't do it. I also don't see how we can have a system where somebody in Washington says no tail fins or bigger fins. Suppose that the man in Washington liked bigger fins than Detroit has. Then what? We have a pluralistic society, and we should structure it so that over a reasonably short period of time enough pressure can be brought to get things changed if the people want a change.

FERRY: How does the pressure work for public parks? You say you cannot set up any non-representative institution, such as the Council of Economic Advisors, which might come out for parks as against lipsticks?

KERR: I was not suggesting the Council of Economic Advisors

as a solution for all problems. Berle mentioned the Council of Economic Advisors in this role. As I said earlier, one small start in what we are talking about would be to get Congress to define national economic health much more broadly than it has. Maybe the American Assembly or somebody should have a conference on the definition of national economic health.

MILLIS: In your definition of national health haven't you got an ideology?

KERR: You would have a goal. At this stage in our national development and the world-wide situation, we need some goals. How we get them in a pluralistic system is the question.

MILLIS: If you have the goals or ideology, then you can go back to planning again.

KERR: It affects planning. But then you would have planning done by many agencies rather than one.

NIEBUHR: Teller mentioned the annual automobile model. Is there any way that in a democratic society the government should say, "Look, we are at peace, but it is almost war, and the annual model is a luxury we can't afford."

HUTCHINS: Ferry raises this question in his paper: What are the possibilities of self-regulation in such a matter as annual models? It might require some amendment in the anti-trust laws or some reinterpretation. Ferry says it would be possible for the automobile industry to get together and agree on the criteria for new models. He suggests what those criteria might be. The criteria are inapplicable to the business at present.

BERLE: Let us take one situation on which economic data are beginning to come in. A couple of years ago the motor industry tooled up and produced something over 8,000,000 cars. They did so in the face of private estimates that the solid market was around 6,000,000, and that they were borrowing from next year's market, and that there would be trouble. So it proved. Actually, sales dropped from 8,200,000 to 4,500,000, or about that. There are people out of jobs, and there were a lot of other miscellaneous repercussions. I would think it would have been possible with some kind of planning mechanism to have worked out a fair estimate and said to everybody, "This is about what you have to work with here. We suggest that if you violate the apparently plain implications of this piece of economics, both you and we are going to be in trouble next year, so don't do it." At this point everybody might say, "All right, we will plan our operation for production of 6,000,000 cars." I would think this could be done on a self-regulated basis to that extent. On other things I don't think it is as simple.

HUTCHINS: Who tells what to whom in the example you have given? Would the government give this advice? Would the government have power to allocate?

BERLE: Yes.

HUTCHINS: So this is a central planning agency that has the power to determine what a large industry is going to do in a given period; is that correct?

BERLE: Yes. I can think of easier ways to do it in that particular case, although we are getting into technical questions. I would have liked to have the Federal Reserve have some power over consumer credit and say, in substance, "If you want to sell 8,000,000 cars, we are not going to try to stop you, but we will say this: that beyond 6,000,000 whoever buys a car will have to do so with his own money. He will not be able to borrow it at the bank or from a finance company."

GOLDMAN: I am still unclear about the extent of powers that any of these bodies is going to have and the exact description of what each is going to do. I can easily see the advisability of having Congress empower one of these bodies to consider the general economic health. It would help create a public consensus in that field. But when it starts going beyond that to try to enforce a definition of economic health, then I run into two objections: that you don't know whether the body is really going to enforce a good kind of economy or not, and we get back to the lipstick business too. Both of those are serious objections to any group with considerable power.

KERR: If you get a consensus in this country, aren't there lots of mechanisms already existing for making it effective?

BERLE: A little too late. This is where I think criticism comes in. The critics should be a little ahead of the people, and they ought to help the public consensus get there a shade ahead of where it does now. If additional powers are needed, this will become apparent as things go along. For example, the need for government power to steer credit away from the stock market became apparent in 1929; the National City Bank said to government: "You mustn't regulate credit. We know better, and you make mistakes." Actually, it was the bank that made the mistake and almost went bankrupt.

FERRY: A critical group would articulate what I consider to be a present consensus, one that Goldman does not think exists. I believe there is at present a pro-park, pro-school, pro-decent public facilities, pro-housing consensus existing in this country. I think this consensus is suffocating underneath the mass media. The lipstick makers can help to suffocate it and hold it out of view by the pressure of advertising. This sort of consensus needs as much articulation as building up at the present time. This would be a main duty of a critical group.

GOLDMAN: If you say you want to set up a planning body that will have the power to act as if this consensus does exist before we know whether it exists or not, then I would wonder about the effectiveness of such a body.

HUTCHINS: The planning group would be a part of society under all the pressures of society, and we can't assume that it is going to outrun the consensus.

NIEBUHR: Aren't we using the word "consensus" too loosely? What, in a democratic society, is consensus? Everything remains a matter of debate. Consensus means overwhelming sentiment for something or other. Ferry talks about the consensus for housing as against lipsticks, and says it is submerged. That means it is not a consensus. There is no real consensus except on survival or something like that.

FERRY: We are in very bad shape if anything that is submerged does not exist. One thing we know from five years of experience in the Fund for the Republic is that there is apparently no concern, as far as one can see, for freedom and justice in this country. Would you say that because they are submerged and unseen they are of no importance and have no part in the American consensus?

HUTCHINS: We can do this perfectly well without the word consensus, can't we? We would all like to have the economy as reasonable as it can be. We all recognize the limitations of human reason. We know we are never going to get a Utopian situation. The sole question is: "How can you make the economic order as rational as it can be?" There has been agreement that some form of institutionalized criticism would be desirable. There was substantial agreement at one stage today that some kind of central planning agency with some kind of authority would be desirable. As I understand you, Goldman, you do not subscribe to the latter view.

GOLDMAN: No.

FERRY: Suppose it were to be set up as proposed in the paper, by legislation?

GOLDMAN: You are now talking about a planning board with authority?

HUTCHINS: Yes.

GOLDMAN: This is not the critical agency which will think about these things, which will argue with the public?

HUTCHINS: No. As I understand it, there is no difference of opinion here about the desirability of institutionalized criticism, recognizing all the difficulties that might arise if we went into it in any detail. On the principle there seems to be no difference. There is a difference on the question of planning with authority. You object to that.

GOLDMAN: I don't know what we mean by it yet. The instances that Berle has given here are fairly minor.

HUTCHINS: Berle suggested that the central agency would have the power to determine whether or not General Motors should make more than X million cars.

BERLE: The public consensus is not whether General Motors should or should not make more cars in a given year. The consensus is that there ought to be a more or less even arrangement so we don't have wide alterations between employment and unemployment. I think there is a consensus on that already, as there is a consensus that we ought not to have monopolies. It is giving direct application to such a consensus and saying what it means in terms of action that is the problem. The first stage, I would think, would be advisory, if you wish. Somebody says the people don't want a lot of unemployment. If you manufacture more than so many cars you are going to get a lot of unemployment and there will be trouble. After a while you might get to the point where this could be crystallized into direct control power such as the Federal Reserve has in connection with the money supply now.

GOLDMAN: Isn't that precisely the point? If an advisory board says to the public year after year, "This year, if you want to be sensible, you make five, and that year, if you want to be sensible, you make seven," the public will begin to get the idea that it is a pretty good notion to have a board of experts saying how many automobiles to make. Then, through the existence of the consensus, they will say to the Federal Reserve Board, "Control it."

HUTCHINS: If you could have a substantial majority in Congress today show that there was a submerged consensus in favor of a central agency with power now, you wouldn't object to it?

GOLDMAN: No.

RABI: Isn't this the theory of the fortune-teller, that she is right a certain number of times? Unless you have an underlying theory that those people could do the right thing, the fact that they were right a few times would not be constructive at all. You have to have an underlying theory or you might as well go to the fortune-teller.

HUTCHINS: As I understand it, we have arrived at agreement on the desirability of institutionalized criticism without prejudice as to the form this institution might take or the subjects that might come under its purview. We have also agreed that if legislation were adopted authorizing a central planning agency, that would be acceptable.

Mr. Goldman has felt that in the absence of such legislation, a central planning agency would be objectionable. His objection is not in principle to a central planning agency, but an objection to a central planning agency in advance of such consensus as would support legislation in this regard.

There is one aspect of the planning problem that you may want to express yourselves on. That is the relationship of planning to technological development, or the problem of the control of technological development and whether that is possible. At a meeting of the advisors to the Corporation Project, Mr. Hacker of Cornell took the position that this was ridiculous. He said there was no way in which you could guide or direct technological development, and you might as well forget about it. Ferry's paper recommends guiding and directing technological development in the public interest, concluding, therefore, that the planning would function.

GOLDMAN: That is the place where it would be most successful.

HUTCHINS: Mr. Hacker's argument was an argument from history. It has never been possible to do this.

MILLIS: My tendency would be to sympathize with Mr. Hacker. It seems impossible to me that this could be brought down to factual and precise statements. What do you mean by guiding technological development?

RABI: It is very difficult. Take the case of EURATOM. Around the time of Suez it was clear that Europe would be dollar-poor and oil-poor and coal-poor, and they thought of atomic-energy development. Now coal is a glut on the market and oil is a glut on the market, and so on. There is a case of long-range planning. It is probably still correct, but it would be awfully difficult to convince people to go on with it. The prognosticators are so poor. If you knew the conditions, and knew the laws of the thing you were discussing, then you could program it like a computing machine. There would be no problem. The only problem you would have is in formulating the desires. Then we would know how to do it.

FERRY: The suggestion was made in the paper that arguing from history would not get us very far because of the kind of developments we have seen in the last few years, the most spectacular of which is the bomb, of course. Other instances given are developments in genetics, developments in the use of drugs. If it is possible for a people totally to change its outlook, let us say, by the use of drugs, the question is what, if anything, should we do about this? Perhaps the analogy with the du Pont chart room is wrong. It is, however, an impressive story.

Du Pont says they are in the business of technology and so they develop and perfect and then hold things off the market until the market is ready to receive them, for commercial and other reasons. The story of holding nylon and dacron off the market until the market could be prepared properly for their reception is a fascinating one.

This may be an imperfect analogy. It is intended to show private planning of technological development. It seems to me, however, that we may have similar situations in other areas, and society ought to take the means of protecting itself or dealing sensibly with technology, which it will not necessarily cope with as successfully tomorrow as it has in the past. The question is:

What do we need to do to live with the technological knowledge now coming into our possession?

MURRAY: Does this include technology as related to war and also the technological development of underdeveloped countries, or is this purely the industrial complex that you are talking about?

FERRY: It takes in all of them.

GOLDMAN: I would like to ask Millis to explain the historical objection.

FERRY: May I remind you that we have already a good deal of regulation and control in this area. The government retains and controls the use of fissionable materials. There will be a great commotion about the public and peaceful uses of atomic materials. It has started already.

MILLIS: I was not making an historical objection. I don't understand, really, what this idea involves. We are all terribly conscious of what technology has done to us. But how are you going to control it? These examples—the du Pont chart room, the control of the AEC over fissionable materials—do not seem to me to begin to go to the heart of what you would have to do. Du Pont has an organization and can control its own actions. But it cannot control the general development of chemistry which is not found in the laboratories of the du Pont Company. The AEC can control the use of fissionable material, but it can't control the development of things like rockets.

FERRY: At first we found some difficulty in controlling patent medicines. We have them under control now. We have done the same thing with food. I suggest that it is not difficult to control technology, as soon as one says, "Yes, the public has an immediate interest in this." But when we say we ought to have some method of appraising technology and keeping it under control, it does not mean to march into the laboratories and say, "Don't investigate; don't get into research." Our concern would be with the social effects of things turned up by research.

MURRAY: The fact that the United States Government owns all fissionable material does not mean that nuclear technology is under control. It is only under control by its own inner dynamism, which consists of doing what can be done. If you want to control technology, I think you have to build controls not out of technology itself. You have to invoke some other discipline which could only be politics in the widest possible sense of the word.

BUCHANAN: You would agree that there is a speculative side to science?

MURRAY: Yes. But the speculative side of these sciences acts as a principle of expansion and not as a principle of control.

FERRY: At an early meeting, Father Murray, you made the comment that military policy is decided by weapons technology and not vice versa. Everybody agreed to that. Would you restate that, and take out the word "military," so that your statement would be "national policy is decided by technology and not vice versa"?

MURRAY: I haven't enough knowledge to make any such sweeping generalization. I have a feeling that the technological has assumed a primacy over policy in some broad sense. We go ahead doing the things we can do because the scientific and technological means of doing them are at hand or within reach. Whether we ought to do them is another question. Why are we doing them; what are the immediate and long-range effects of doing this or that? These are questions that by and large we don't attend to very much.

FERRY: This is the heart of the proposal: that we should pause to consider, and to ask these questions of technology, and find some way of controlling it.

KERR: I don't have very much to say about this except to say it is absolutely impossible. If it were possible, it would be highly unwise.

FERRY: Mustn't we deal with automation? We deal with it in secondary effects. After a man is laid off, we train him or pay him unemployment insurance.

110

KERR: When you say that, you should stop. Technology and science and thought are all tied together. When you say you want to control technology, you are saying you want to control new ideas. This is one of the greatest potential attacks on freedom of thought I have ever heard about.

HUTCHINS: Suppose we said we were for the orderly introduction of the application of new ideas.

KERR: I don't know that they ever have been introduced in an orderly way. If we start to introduce them in an orderly way, somebody would introduce them in a disorderly way and get a long way ahead of us.

BUCHANAN: Isn't it important to understand new ideas?

KERR: That is a different thing.

BUCHANAN: That is the emphasis I was putting on it. Before you begin to exercise social control, it is very important to understand these things. We are not understanding them at present.

GOLDMAN: Isn't the trouble with the control part? I take this proposal to mean not control, although the word "control" is being used. The public appraisal of the potential social utility of technological advances would appear to be needed.

JACOBS: The greatest technological development in the movement of oil came when some guy, fooling around in the cellar, figured out a way of introducing camphor balls into the pipeline to perform a function that had been performed before by a pumping station. There are many ways in which you can interfere with the development of technology. In England, for example, the trade unions consciously interfere with the development of technology and by so doing manage to keep productivity down.

RABI: To get an orderly introduction.

KERR: That is right. It is a terrible thing.

FERRY: Is there something virtuous in itself in adopting a technological improvement that will lay off workers?

JACOBS: If I have to judge this for virtue or fault, I would say that introduction of technological improvements is virtuous if you believe that the standard of living ought to increase and that the physical aspects of work ought to be lessened. The suggestion implicit here, I take it, is that we will resist the development of technological change unless it is possible to introduce it in an orderly way. I don't see how you can, because it is devised in a disorderly way.

FERRY: There are methods of introducing automation in an orderly manner, and not in the manner in which it has been introduced. The methods rest on an appraisal and understanding of the potential good and evils in the process. It says that the evils would be too swift firing, displacement of thousands of workers. Therefore we will automate slowly. We will tell employees where they can go, we will train them for new jobs. This is what the proposal means.

JACOBS: The reason you exercise control is that in the absence of control you think you will have evil consequences. We don't control just for the sake of control.

RABI: Suppose you have something which has some of the effects of technology, but which is just a matter of nature; for example, the dry period and the dust bowl. I always think of the effects of technology as I do of other natural things. Events occur. Land goes bad, fashions change. Suddenly the hansom cab driver is out of work. Often it has nothing to do with technology. Are you really saying any more than that you would like to see more forethought in society than meeting problems as they come? Technology supplies a number of them but perhaps not even the greatest number.

FERRY: I would accept most of that.

GOLDMAN: Ferry is saying that there should be a kind of technological watchdog—

RABI: Ferry is for setting up a group to put a brake on changes.

It may be a good idea. I think what he is talking about is as extensive as that. It is not just technology.

JACOBS: We are in the midst of a technological revolution involving food. The entire production and processing and marketing of food has changed as a result of the packaging devices that are now used in the sheds. You can not go easily into a produce market today and buy a head of lettuce or a bunch of carrots that is not wrapped in cellophane. I deplore this, because I like to poke my carrots.

KELLY: Other people don't like to buy them after you poke them.

JACOBS: Right. That is one reason why they are now wrapped in cellophane. They literally move in a packing shed and vacuum pack into the field, and out comes the lettuce. This has wiped out what was once a huge and flourishing business in the United States, the commission produce people. The big markets are ghost towns. The produce goes right from the grower to the big supermarket.

In this case I think society is losing something, but the fashion is for easy cooking. Part of the fashion is the television dinner. Part is the fact that you don't have cooks or domestic servants any longer. The best thing that can happen is that at some point we should take a good look at this process. There ought to be some way of taking the people whose livelihoods have been affected and getting them into some other line of work.

HUTCHINS: One of the reasons why the vegetables are wrapped in cellophane is that the du Pont Company reorganized most of the vegetable growing in the United States so that everything would be wrapped in cellophane. In other words, du Pont was engaged in the kind of technological planning and appraisal that perhaps ought to have been done simultaneously by the public. It seems to me our discussion has been largely concerned with straw monsters. I don't understand that Ferry is proposing anything more than what you have just suggested if you apply it to the industrial system and technology as a whole.

GOLDMAN: I personally see no objection to it. But there is a tendency on our part to be solving all problems by setting up a commission to serve as a kind of watchdog. We will have one to watch the corporation and one to watch technology. This could tend to be a fairly superficial solution of these problems.

FERRY: The statement says that some kind of public control of the most dangerous developments of technology would appear to be indispensable, but I am not aware that any commission for this has been suggested. Some methods of control used at present are mentioned. Du Pont has one way of controlling technology. The International Labor Office helps through publicity. Out of such examples as these it may be possible to erect the rudiments of a control system. I do not think that it would be possible to set up a central bureau, to which technologists would repair and say, "How about this?" Other kinds of intermediate agencies might play some part. I am not sure what has to be done. First, what you have to do is to say there is a problem.

HUTCHINS: When you get into almost any public question, the issue is, shall this social phenomenon be allowed to run wild? Is the best answer essentially that of "bumps and grinds"? Or shall you control it, which has to be by governmental action? The reason why commissions are recommended often is not because they are easy, but because the only alternative between letting things run wild and controlling them through government action is criticism of some sort. This is one of the things that is grossly lacking in the United States as compared with England, where the tradition of the Royal Commission is established and under which many useful services have been performed. Take the question of the press. You can't control it. It is clearly irresponsible at the present time. What can you do about it? About all you can do, it seems to me, is to try to imagine the best type of continuing appraisal of it.

KERR: There is a lot of difference between a Royal Commission and having some mechanism for controlling the monstrous evils of technology. The great advantage of the Royal Commission is that it goes out of business.

HUTCHINS: You might have a Royal Commission on automation at one stage, and it might go out of business. If the situation changes, you might have another in another sector. I don't see that there is anything in Ferry's proposal that would exclude the possibility of a series of Royal Commissions.

GOLDMAN: You are not leading to compulsion.

BUCHANAN: This is the way the government works now.

HOFFMAN: When you get people to do things or not do things by talking about that or persuading, isn't this control in a sense?

KERR: Influence is different from control.

GOLDMAN: May I come back a moment to the defense of Royal Commissions? I would repeat my uneasiness that we are not getting to the root of the problem when we apply the idea of commissions across the board. That is our tendency here with respect to corporations and technology.

KELLY: What you are advocating is no action at all.

GOLDMAN: No. Each one of these commissions that would be set up would be that much less effective, because you would have a whole chorus of voices sounding out.

KERR: It seems to me we might some time have a discussion on how you control the control mechanism. It seems to me that there ought to be some real study of how you get control mechanisms to control the people they are supposed to control rather than somebody else. The Railroad Commissions end up by aiding the railroads and protecting them against the public. You have a hundred illustrations, I think, of where the control agency ends up as the protector.

KELLY: This is in the case of government commissions. What about citizen commissions?

KERR: I don't know. I want to throw this in as a subject for discussion some time.

HUTCHINS: This comes up in the project on the political process. It also is an important aspect of Goldman's project on the mass media. The most glaring example of what you speak of is in that field.

KERR: It is also how you structure government itself. It is not just the political mechanism of legislation but how you structure the civil service; what subject matters you cover; how many different people are able to bring pressure upon the same agency. Do you have a conflict of interest in the agency or only one group that comes in control? As we are moving to more control by the government, there ought to be more strategy on the part of the public for the control of these agencies so they don't do the opposite of what they are intended to do.

KELLY: Goldman, what would you say if the press had the maturity to engage in really searching self-criticism?

GOLDMAN: That would be ideal.

KELLY: The trouble is they are unwilling to do this. *The New York Times* says that it feels as a newspaper it should not criticize the press, and that criticism of the press should come from an outside agency such as the Fund for the Republic.

GOLDMAN: You are agreeing with what we are saying. We are saying that outside criticism is useful. But is this a basic solution to the problem of technology?

KELLY: What other way have you of getting at basic solutions except disinterested criticism?

GOLDMAN: We have not gone very far when we have said that.

BUCHANAN: Under your theory, don't you have a solution, that is, to set up your pressure groups?

GOLDMAN: Yes. But the more of them you set up, the less effective they are. Kerr's objection was to a control board, with which I agree. Now this is raising the question of the importance of a non-control board.

BUCHANAN: Do you pluralists recognize the danger of the pressure groups?

GOLDMAN: Yes.

BUCHANAN: It seems to me the dangers are much greater in that field than in the possibility of commissions taking over. We believe in self-government somehow. The pressure groups do not. They are fighting.

GOLDMAN: They are fighting for approval by the voter.

BUCHANAN: I am not sure it is approval. They want to win a battle.

MILLIS: I am uncertain about what we are talking about when we are talking about control of technology. We are speaking of two controls. One would control the impact of technology on the social structure and provide for people thrown out by automation, for example. The other is the control of the impact of technology not on just one group of workers but upon the whole shape of our lives. I don't know any answer to Kerr's argument that this latter form of control is impossible. I don't see how it can be done. If Ferry or anybody else has an idea of how it could be done, I would like to see it.

FERRY: I said earlier I am unable to describe anything except instances where control has been made effective already. I would not care to try to improvise now. Consider the fact that for over 150 years we have protected the technologists, the patentees, through the Patent Office. We have been very careful to protect their rights and property. But when the reverse proposition is made to protect the people against the possible ill effects of dangerous, influential, powerful technological developments, this somehow seems to be a suggestion of a different order. Scientists report to us about certain audio waves being able to kill a pig or a monkey at a certain wave length. We won't have any trouble reaching agreement on the control of such waves, will we?

GOLDMAN: May I try to state one thing that bothers me? Something like the smog situation in Los Angeles brings up the real difficulty in this situation, namely, that the American people do not understand the workings of their own society. They do not understand how a pressure group here or there has brought about the smog. They don't understand why if they gave the money to someone, he could not hire people to get rid of it. This seems to me to be a much more basic statement than the mere suggestion of a commission. I realize that all I am doing is resorting to the age-old proposition that if the American people were perfectly educated, they would have a good society. But what is our function unless we perhaps are willing to state banal things which may happen to be true, rather than get swept away with what I suspect could be a little gadgeteering on our part, like suggesting a commission to get that smog solved?

FERRY: But you have evidence that things can be done. The great technological accomplishment of the East Coast, this mammoth snarl called New York City and environs, something sensible could be made out of this. The city is going to be here. It will not go away. Things are getting worse. This does not mean that something could not be done.

KERR: In terms of technology over-all, it would be absolutely impossible to do anything about it. Let us grant it does some horrible things to society. It also does some wonderful things. Technology is so all-pervasive that you could not have a commission on technology to do anything about it. As individual things come along, as the automobile came along, you do start certain rules for their use. You can tackle certain aspects of new technological developments where they get out of line with the public interest. But to talk about some kind of a commission to study technology over-all or some government commission to control technology over-all is absolutely impossible. This thing was unleashed on the world. It is going to keep on growing. We have no idea what the ultimate consequences are going to be. I don't know how you would ever tackle it. I think you can say that as things come along which may seem unfortunate to humanity, humanity will take them up one at a time. I don't see how you can look at the problem over-all.

HUTCHINS: I call your attention to the fact that technology is controlled (a) by government and (b) by industry, and this is a very hit-or-miss affair. For example, in the field of television, it would appear that for reasons of their own, such things as ultra high frequencies, which could make whole new areas available, are suppressed by the industry. Color television is in a very ambiguous position. So is FM radio. In this one field there are three technological problems of the greatest importance, and the benefits that might flow from them are inhibited by non-rational considerations and by the assumed financial interests of those who control the business.

RABI: Business said there should be an orderly introduction.

HUTCHINS: What the business said was that there should be an orderly non-introduction.

KERR: That is what orderly introduction usually means; it means non-introduction. It usually has meant that in the trade union movement.

JACOBS: Isn't it possible that the necessity is to educate people to demand better uses of their technology? We are substituting the commission for this process of education.

KELLY: Why couldn't the commission be an educational instrument?

JACOBS: There are a variety of educational instruments that operate in society.

HUTCHINS: As I understand it, we are to think about technology as an aspect of the general problem of organizing the economic

119

order. We agreed on an agency of criticism and we agreed on planning, subject to some qualifications. I don't see how technological developments can be omitted from this.

RABI: Some group looking at the society and trying to understand it is fine. We are all trying to do that, in the universities, in the Ford Foundation, the Fund for the Republic, and many other places such as the Twentieth Century Fund. We are trying to understand our society. There are many areas in which technology has been introduced and the race has not yet found good experience to cope with. We must observe the Russian experiment with great interest, because they presumably have the means of control built into the system, to see whether it actually works. But I can't see how the particular suggestion that was made here would work out.

FERRY: The whole proposition for appraisal and control of technology is built on Kerr's statement that technology is the pervasive fact of our lives. I prefer to think that we should remain in control of our own lives, and that technology should not take over.

RABI: Technology can't take over. I don't know how you personify this. You are talking about people who are pressing to do certain technological or other innovations or the effect of natural phenomena, like the melting of the polar ice cap, the warming of the oceans. These things will be happening and people will be doing things with them.

FERRY: Would you dispute Father Murray's statement that weapons technology decides our military policy?

RABI: Certainly. Our military policy is decided by natural objectives within the confines of what we can do. But our national objectives decide our military policy. We don't have to indulge in a cold war with Russia. We could just say, "We will join you." To begin with, there is a certain national purpose, and then the military technology gives the means for doing it. Not only ours, but theirs. Once you look at it in that way, it is clear that we are not free agents. Once you decide a certain line of action, you are not free agents, just as if you were in business.

MILLIS: Any decision of such a commission or so on would have to be political in the large sense.

RABI: In the framework of a political-social objective of some kind.

FERRY: That is the basis of the suggestion in the paper—to try to make social inventions requiring far greater skill and imagination than anything that is so far proposed.

RABI: In a limited field you can make production agreements with other countries. We do it all the time. But when you talk about technology, you talk about all the changes that occur in society because of the way natural laws, human ingenuity, and natural phenomena impinge. Then I think you are really talking about a highly controlled society. The reason we are against it is because we don't believe there is enough wisdom to be found in people who will do it.

KELLY: But don't we believe that a number of nations, for example, will develop hydrogen and similar bombs in the near future?

RABI: It is possible.

KELLY: We think the technology is spreading so that they will be able to do it.

RABI: We are doing our best to spread it.

KELLY: Aren't a number of scientists advocating that we try to control this technology by reaching certain agreements?

RABI: In a limited field, yes.

KELLY: In that sense they are making an effort to do something about technology.

RABI: That is a different thing from the other. You have to do it. But that is not just the technology. All human action where you fabricate or do something is technology. Driving a car is technology. We have speed laws and all sorts of things. In fact, that is what most of the business of our government is, regulation. Technology is being regulated.